Healing
—the—
Heart

Healing
the
Heart

*Helping Your Child Thrive
After Trauma*

Christine Fonseca

PRUFROCK PRESS INC.
WACO, TEXAS

Library of Congress Control Number:2019957625

Copyright ©2020, Prufrock Press Inc.

Edited by Katy McDowall

Cover design by Micah Benson and layout design by Shelby Charette

ISBN-13: 978-1-61821-895-7

Printed in the United States of America.

At the time of this book's publication, all facts and figures cited are the most current available. All telephone numbers, addresses, and website URLs are accurate and active. All publications, organizations, websites, and other resources exist as described in the book, and all have been verified. The authors and Prufrock Press Inc. make no warranty or guarantee concerning the information and materials given out by organizations or content found at websites, and we are not responsible for any changes that occur after this book's publication. If you find an error, please contact Prufrock Press Inc.

Prufrock Press Inc.
P.O. Box 8813
Waco, TX 76714-8813
Phone: (800) 998-2208
Fax: (800) 240-0333
http://www.prufrock.com

Dedication

Dedicated to everyone who has experienced traumatic events, whether due to adverse childhood experiences, natural disasters, community violence, or other events that threaten your very existence. Let the words in this book be a guide, pointing the way to a happy and integrated life in which your stories of trauma result in strength, growth, and resilience.

Table of Contents

Acknowledgments ───────────────

Writing about the impact of trauma has been near and dear to my heart for more than 3 decades, when the impact of my own wounds became all too clear. Now, with the help of the people below and numerous others, the book is finally written. Thank you to my family, friends, colleagues, and the community who supported every word and every page:

To my partner, my husband, my soulmate—once again, your support for my need to express myself in words allows me to live in this creative space. You continually step up and help with the chores, the errands, and the basic necessities of life, even when I forget about everything but writing. You listen to my endless conversations about my various book topics with interest and amusement. You're my strength when I struggle, my consoler when I fail, and my cheer squad when I succeed. Without you, none of this would happen. Thank you for more words, more books, and your endless love and support.

To my amazing children, Fabiana and Erika—you find ways into every book I write. You are examples of living a creative life and my constant source of inspiration. Thank you for being examples of strength, safety, and positivity.

To Katy McDowall and the team at Prufrock Press—you have been my partner now for more than a decade. Together we've created quality books that make the world a better place. Thank you for always listening to my crazy ideas and taking a chance. You have made all of my nonfiction work possible.

To my colleagues at Collaborative Learning Solutions—the work we do has inspired every page of this book. The CLS vision to disrupt the status quo, relentlessly support children in the margins, and make the world a better place for everyone inspires me daily. Thank you for your contributions to this book's content. More importantly, thank you for including me on the crazy ride and allowing me to blend the myriad creative endeavors into a beautiful life.

To the hundreds of contributors around the world—your experiences shaped every page of this book. You shared your thoughts and stories with me online, via e-mail, over Zoom, and in person, and changed my views about trauma and moving from surviving to thriving. Thank you for your collective wisdom and engaging in my book research process so generously. Your stories are nothing short of inspirational.

And finally, to my tribe: the writing community of bloggers, readers, and fans that continue to support and inspire my work—although I only know most of you through online communities, our connections are real and feed my soul. You get me through the hard times, encouraging and supporting the projects waiting to be finished. You champion my work, sharing great stories and offering suggestions for new material. Without you, my stories and self-help books would never take shape or be birthed into the world. I am blessed to share my creative soul with each of you.

Thank you!

—Christine Fonseca

Author's Note

Over the last several years, readers and workshop participants have asked me to address the topic of trauma and toxic stress. It is a frequent news topic and something that is on people's minds. And with good reason. The impact of trauma is significant, often blocking growth and development, and creating barriers for children and adults alike.

Most of the conversations I've seen around trauma focus on adverse childhood experiences (ACEs), including neglect and abuse, mental health issues in the family, and divorce. Seldom do people talk about the impact of war, community violence, and natural disasters, like the devastating California wildfires or hurricanes Harvey and Maria. This more global view of trauma—and the similar impact these events have to ACEs—has consumed my thoughts for several years. I needed to understand all of the ways our stress response becomes maladaptive and toxic. I needed to explore the many ways parents and educators could help children. And I needed to share this information as widely as I could.

Healing the Heart is the outcome of my study. It is a culmination of years of research and practice working with those impacted by trauma, including myself and my family.

Healing the Heart is part parenting book, part self-help book, part workbook. My goal is to provide parents, as well as educators, with the information to best understand what happens when the brain becomes overwhelmed and one's stress response shifts from adaptive to maladaptive. It is designed to give you—the reader—the tools needed to recognize and heal the impact of your personal trauma, if applicable, and best support the children in your life through post-traumatic recovery.

Take time to read the book thoroughly. Do the exercises, especially the reflection work. Then, use the information in your work with children—either as a parent, educator, or another support person. Traumatic events are significant and impact people over an entire lifespan. This doesn't mean the impact is destined to be negative, however. There are ways to repair physical, emotional, and psychological damage. This book will hopefully help you through the process.

Note that *Healing the Heart* is not a substitute for the therapeutic process any more than any self-help book can be. It is simply meant to support you on your journey to understanding the role of trauma in your life and in the lives of the children you know.

Please reach out if you have any questions. Happy reading!

Introduction ———————————

In September 2017, I led a workshop for educators in Houston, TX, less than a month after Hurricane Harvey. The devastation was palpable—not just because of the roads and highways that were under construction, or the dampness that seemed to permeate everything. It was the feelings of fear, panic, and shock that were most startling to me. Everywhere I went, people looked shell-shocked. They were functioning, sort of. But there was an emptiness in their eyes. It was that look that made me stop to change the presentation I was giving to include the impact of trauma and toxic stress on the brain.

Traumatic events can be caused by adverse childhood experiences, devastating natural disasters, community violence, war, and anything that overwhelms one's coping abilities. When one's stress response is bombarded with repeated crises, it can shift from adaptive to maladaptive to toxic. Internal threat centers begin to see danger around every corner. One's body launches into a near-permanent state of fight-or-flight. Blood vessels restrict, cortisol and adrenaline levels elevate, and a host of other physiological responses designed to ensure survival engage. These responses are not meant to last long term. When they do, one's body works against itself and causes damage instead of protection.

In addition to the physiological responses, one's brain locks down as well. The affected individual switches to familiar patterns of behavior that have kept them safe previously, even when the behaviors are negative or maladaptive. Their thinking slows as they turn to pure survival mode.

Linear time loses meaning, and rational thought deteriorates. Their brain and body work for only one thing—survival by any means necessary.

This is a human under the influence of complex trauma. This was what I saw in the eyes of those impacted by Hurricane Harvey. It is the same look I've seen in the eyes of an abused child. And it is what I saw in the eyes of friends just after the 9/11 attacks in New York. It is also what I've seen in the mirror at various times of my own life.

Healing the Heart: Helping Your Child Thrive After Trauma was written to address the impact of trauma on human functioning. It begins by defining the types of trauma children experience; the effect of these experiences on the body, brain, emotions, and behaviors; and finally, how to best support children through and beyond their stories of trauma.

How to Use This Book

Healing the Heart is part informational, part workbook. The first half (Parts I and II) focuses on defining trauma and its impact. Part I focuses on identifying the many types of trauma events children experience. Chapter 1 discusses adverse childhood experiences, or ACEs, and Felitti et al.'s (1998) groundbreaking research into the impact of ACEs over the lifespan. Chapter 2 expands the conversation about traumatic events to include natural disasters, community violence, war, and other significant events. Chapter 3 discusses the human stress response and how traumatic events can push that response from healthy to unhealthy to toxic.

In Part II, the impact of trauma on children is explored more deeply. Chapter 5 examines neurobiology and trauma, looking for specific ways trauma impacts neurological functioning. Chapter 6 reviews the research regarding the effect of trauma and toxic stress on emotions and behavior. Additional attention is given to the impact of trauma with unique populations, including members of the LGBTQ community or children who are neurologically diverse.

The second half of the book switches from information to strategies designed to help children move through the traumatic experience and thrive. Part III provides a foundation of healing by examining the ways to rebuild safety for children. Chapter 9 lays a necessary foundation for security at home and school. Chapter 10 discusses the importance of healthy relationships in repairing and healing the minds and bodies of children. Chapter 11 provides strategies to help children and families move past traumatic events.

In Part IV, you will learn how to regain hope and optimism after the traumatic events. Chapter 12 focuses on thriving at home, while Chapters 13 and 14 extend the hope into the school and the broader community settings. Each of these chapters includes "Frequently Asked Questions" that cover a variety of topics provided by parents and educators during my many workshops, coaching sessions, or online conversations.

Chapters also include highlighted topics that cover the role of mass media in perpetuating traumatic responses, how technology influences a traumatic response, and the role of resiliency, to name a few. Chapters end with "Healing the Heart," a section that recaps the big ideas and provides recommended action steps to help heal the harmful effects of trauma for the whole family.

Finally, *Healing the Heart* includes stories from trauma-impacted children, adolescents, and adults. Through these stories, the effects of trauma come to life. These stories also illustrate many of the strategies and tips offered throughout the book.

As I mentioned earlier, *Healing the Heart* is part informational, part workbook. It is designed to be interactive. Each chapter includes reflection exercises, tips, questionnaires, and activities for you and your children to complete. The more you lean into the various exercises in the book, the more you gain.

A Note to Educators

Although *Healing the Heart* is geared for parents, sections of the book are applicable to educators and mental health support staff. Every chapter in Parts I–III includes a special section called "Trauma-Informed Practices." These sections highlight specific information related to children impacted by trauma and how to assist them within the school setting. Topics include how ACEs affect the classroom, the impact of school shootings, and decoding behavior. Specific strategies and tips are presented through each section. These strategies are also engaging and informative for parents as their children navigate the school setting. Parents may also find these sections useful for developing talking points for conversations with educators about their child's post-trauma recovery.

In addition to the specialized sections in each chapter, Chapter 13: Thriving at School addresses ways for schools to be more trauma-sensitive and trauma-informed. Resources and educationally-focused "Frequently Asked Questions" sections provide teachers and support personnel what they need to best help students impacted by traumatic events. The stories that end each part of the book also highlight ways that schools can help students.

A Little Warning

This is a book about trauma. Many of the examples, stories, and topics have the potential to trigger memories related to traumatic events. Although care was given to be minimally graphic in the discussion of traumatic events, this is a highly emotional topic. If at any time you find yourself in psychological distress as a result of the book, stop. Take a breath and center your thinking. A strong response could be a sign of additional work you may need to do around your own story of trauma. I encourage you to explore those emotions, determine your needs, and get further support if it is needed. When you are able, come back to the book. Finish it. Use the information to help yourself and the children in your life.

Part I
From ACEs to Natural Disasters
Understanding the Impact of Traumatic Events

Trauma and adverse childhood experiences, or ACEs, have permeated the news over the last few years. The medical and education communities have become more and more aware of the impact of traumatic events and the corresponding toxic levels of stress on the developing minds and bodies of children. Researchers have discovered not only that trauma is significantly more common than anyone suspected, but also that its impact on the lifespan of an individual is broader and deeper than previously realized.

Yet, despite increased research and awareness about trauma, average parents (and teachers, too) remain unsure as to the best ways to help their children. Furthermore, most of the investigation into trauma limits the definitions of traumatic events to those adverse experiences occurring within the home, including neglect, abuse, and drug involvement.

This section explores a more in-depth view of trauma, including not only adverse childhood experiences, but also the potentially traumatic impact of natural disasters, community violence, and world events. Additionally, this section begins to explore why traumatic events impact the developing brain and bodies of children and what you can do to help.

Part I ends with the first of four stories, written to illustrate the impact of trauma and the capacity of humans to overcome even the most difficult of situations. In this story, a trauma-impacted adult discusses the upside to her experiences with trauma and how she moved from afraid to fearless.

Chapter 1
The Impact of Adverse Childhood Experiences

♡
___

Trauma has become a common term in today's world, describing everything from horrifying events to getting yelled at by a teacher. In truth, trauma refers to specific events that overpower a person's coping mechanisms. As you can guess based on the definition, people may experience potentially traumatizing events in different ways. Some may be unaffected or minimally impacted by the events, whereas others may be overwhelmed. Each person's experiences of potentially traumatizing situations are influenced by the developmental stage of the person, their social-emotional competencies (especially in the area of resilience), as well as cultural beliefs.

Rice and Groves (2005) defined trauma as "an exceptional experience in which powerful and dangerous events overwhelm a person's capacity to cope" (p. 3). This is, perhaps, the most complete definition I've read and is the meaning I am using when I refer to trauma, trauma stories, and traumatic events through this book.

Trauma can be caused by many different types of events, ranging from abuse, to devastating natural disasters, to community violence, including mass shootings, acts of terrorism, or war. Traumatic events happen within a contextual setting. This means that the scope and impact of trauma can include a collective community experience, even transmitting across generations (St. Andrews, 2013).

Trauma has the potential to change people's brains and bodies in a variety of ways. Experiencing repeated incidences of traumatic events can not only impact your brain, but also change the way in which your brain may function, resulting in differences in your thinking, emotional experiences, and behaviors.

This chapter is about one of the most common forms of traumatic experiences—adverse childhood experiences, or ACEs. ACEs and their impact have been increasingly researched over the past 20 years, starting with the landmark study from Felitti et al. in 1998. This study revealed that ACEs are more common than previously thought and have significant negative impacts throughout a person's lifetime. Ongoing research has yielded similar results, with clearer explanations of the impacts of ACEs on the developing brains and bodies of children and adults.

ACEs Defined

Felitti et al. (1998) researched ACEs extensively, discovering the significant impact ACEs have on the developing brains and bodies of children over a lifetime. The Australian Childhood Foundation (2018) referred to the trauma caused by ACEs as developmental trauma, due to the impact found on overall development and functioning of children. Before I discuss the impact of ACEs and the resultant trauma, I must define both of the types of experiences defined as ACEs and their prevalence.

ACEs have been defined as including abuse—physical, emotional, and sexual—physical and emotional neglect, exposure to alcohol or drug use within the home, exposure to a household member who has a significant mental health condition (i.e., emotional disturbance, suicidal ideations, serious depression), incarceration of a household member, parental separation or divorce, and domestic abuse. Since the original study (Felitti et al., 1998), the definition of ACEs has expanded to include community and school violence, natural disasters, and acts of terrorism and war. The latter events are discussed more in Chapter 2.

Two landmark studies of ACEs point to a high prevalence of exposure to ACEs. In the Felitti et al. (1998) study, findings indicated that 70% of participants experienced at least one ACE (an ACE score of 1), with 87% of those participants experiencing more than one ACE. Findings also indicated a direct correlation between high ACE scores and early smoking and sexual behavior, as well as increased adolescent pregnancy and partner violence. According to the study, participants with an ACE score of 4 or more had significantly increased risk rates for emphysema, chronic bronchitis, depression, and suicide. Similar findings have been noted in more than a dozen additional studies across 18 states.

Another landmark study was the comprehensive national survey on children's exposure to violence conducted by the Department of Justice and Centers for Disease Control and Prevention (Finkelhor et al., 2009). This study evaluated more than 4,500 children from birth to age 17. Results indicated that more than 60% of participants had been exposed to violence in the home, school, or community. More than 38% of participants had been victimized two or more times, and more than 10% had been victimized more than four times. The most common forms of violence the children were exposed to were experiencing physical assault and witnessing assault within the community or home.

Based on both the definition of ACEs and their prevalence, you can see that the experience of trauma is significantly more widespread than originally understood. As you begin to examine you and/or your child's exposure to trauma, start with Worksheet 1: Understanding My Trauma and Its Impact. Complete the first part of the worksheet and determine ACE scores for you and your children. You can use any of the available surveys listed.

The Impact of ACEs

Now that you understand the types of experiences included in the definition of ACEs and the prevalence of exposure to those experiences, you must understand the impact of ACEs. As mentioned previously, the research has linked ACEs to a number of short- and long-term neg-

Worksheet 1
Understanding My Trauma and Its Impact

Part 1

Directions: Complete an ACE survey for you and your children, and determine your ACE score. Use any of the resources below:

- ACE Questionnaire from the National Council of Juvenile and Family Court Judges: https://www.ncjfcj.org/sites/default/files/Finding%20 Your%20ACE%20Score.pdf
- Got Your ACE Score? from Aces Too High: https://acestoohigh.com/ got-your-ace-score
- The ACEs Quiz from NPR: https://www.npr.org/sections/health-shots/ 2015/03/02/387007941/take-the-ace-quiz-and-learn-what-it-does-and-doesnt-mean

Score: _____

Part 2

Based on the chapter and Table 1: The Impact of Trauma, list the potential ways trauma has impacted you or your children.

Physical impact: _____

_____

_____

_____

_____

_____

Cognitive impact: _____

_____

_____

_____

_____

_____

_____

Emotional impact: _____

_____

_____

_____

_____

_____

_____

Social/behavioral impact: _____

_____

_____

_____

_____

_____

_____

ative health outcomes (Felitti et al., 1998). These negative outcomes include immediate injury, neurobiological impairments, increased risky behaviors, significant long-term social behaviors, and major disease and disability.

Several immediate injuries can occur from physical abuse and neglect. These injuries include burns, fractures, traumatic brain injuries, and disrupted cognitive and physical development. Each of these can impact long-term physical and emotional functioning. Neurobiological effects of trauma caused by ACEs include poor emotional regulation, impaired cognitive development, mental health concerns, impaired memory, and somatic concerns. Increased risky behaviors include smoking, drug and alcohol use, self-injurious behaviors and suicidal ideations, risky sexual behavior, and eating disorders. In the long term, the neurobiological impact and risky behaviors can result in many serious social issues, including homelessness, delinquent and violent behaviors, employment issues, compromised adult functioning, retraumatization, and intergenerational trauma.

Perhaps some of the most astounding information from the original ACEs study (Felitti et al., 1998) is the correlation between exposure to traumatic events in childhood and later disease development. The study found links between high ACE scores and cancer, lung disease, diabetes, and ischemic heart disease (Burke Harris, 2018). Clearly, the impact of trauma exposure is significant.

The impact of trauma is influenced by several factors, including the amount of exposure. Research indicates that the higher the amount of exposure to ACEs, the bigger the potential impact. Children who experience chronic trauma—defined as multiple events over an extended period of time—typically experience a greater negative impact. Table 1 highlights many of the areas affected by chronic trauma exposure. Use this table as you consider the potential impact of ACEs to you and your family. Then, complete the second part of Worksheet 1: Understanding My Trauma and Its Impact (p. 10).

Table 1

The Impact of Trauma

Physical	Cognitive	Emotional	Social/Behavioral
• Hyperarousal • Poor appetite • Gastrointestinal issues • Somatic complaints • Increased threat perception • Sleep disturbances • Long-term major illness development	• Nightmares • Distorted and intrusive thought patterns • Decreased self-esteem • Poor decision making • Memory impairments • Increases in worry and anxious-like behaviors • Poor attention and concentration skills	• Phobia development • Increased fears and terrors • Shock • Emotional numbing and dissociation • Helplessness • Increases in sadness and depression-like behaviors • Hypersensitivity and increased emotional intensity	• Work and school impairments • Social isolation • Increased conflicts • Increases in risky behaviors • Increased aggression and violent behaviors • Regression in emotional development • School and work refusal

Supporting Children Impacted by ACEs

Many of the negative health outcomes occur as a result of ineffective coping strategies. Drug and alcohol use, poor eating habits and lifestyle choices, and immature social-emotional skills often occur as children attempt to help themselves survive the trauma. Food, sex, and substance abuse become ways to detach from their feelings, numb themselves, or reduce tension. Sometimes, children see no connection between their behaviors and the trauma they have experienced (Biere & Lanktree, 2011). This is where you can help your child. Remaining curious about your child's behavior, understanding that the maladaptive coping strategies you may be observing can be related to the trauma, and believing that you can positively impact your child and improve their outcomes is an important foundation.

In order to best support children who are experiencing a negative impact from ACEs, first ensure that you have support. Talking with your child about trauma is difficult. Make sure you aren't going through this alone. Regular connections with your support system will ensure that you are able to best support your child.

Once you have established personal support, there are several things you can do to support children impacted by trauma. Begin by learning about toxic stress, chronic trauma, and the types of reactions children often demonstrate. Part II of this book will help. Focus on establishing safety first and foremost. Your child needs both physical and psychological safety in order to heal. Make sure they understand how their safety is ensured. Chapter 9 goes into more detail about establishing safety.

In addition to providing safety, allow your child to freely express their fears. Reassure them that they are not responsible for what has happened. Be willing to talk about their fears and help them process through them. Enlist the help of a mental health professional if your child's emotional distress continues or increases. The school and your medical doctor can be good sources for a referral. Table 2 highlights the general ways to support children impacted by ACEs and includes the specific tip sheets, worksheets, and charts in this book that address each area.

ACEs With iGen and Gen Alpha

Today's children are experiencing decreases in self-esteem, increases in anxiety and depression, and increases in suicidal ideations at an alarming rate (Stiglic & Viner, 2019). Based on research about iGen (defined as children born between 1996 and 2012), technology and increased screen-time are correlated to some negative outcomes, including reduced social-emotional learning skills, reduced happiness, and increased anxiety and depression (Twenge & Campbell, 2018; Twenge et al., 2018). As technology use continues to increase with Generation Alpha (children born after 2012), one can assume that the negative mental health outcomes may continue.

Table 2

Supporting Children Impacted by ACEs

Area of Support	Tip Sheets, Worksheets, and Charts
Education About Trauma and Toxic Stress	• Tip Sheet 18: Deescalating Students (p. 153) • Worksheet 1: Understanding My Trauma (p. 10) • Worksheet 2: Potentially Traumatizing Events (p. 23) • Table 1: The Impact of Trauma (p. 13) • Table 3: A Continuum of Trauma (p. 34) • Table 4: Symptoms of Toxic Stress (p. 35)
Creating a Sense of Safety and Belonging	• Tip Sheet 8: Psychological Safety at Home (p. 95) • Tip Sheet 19: Strategies for Successful Circles (p. 156) • Table 8: Creating a Network of Support (p. 154)
Developing Self-Regulation Skills	• Tip Sheet 6: Keeping a Behavior Journal (p. 68) • Tip Sheet 11: Mindfulness Practice (p. 106) • Worksheet 7: Correcting Thought Patterns (p. 107) • Table 5: Understanding Behavior (p. 67) • Table 6: Decoding Behavior (p. 70)
Building Resiliency Skills	• Tip Sheet 7: Developing Emotional Literacy (p. 88) • Tip Sheet 9: Building SEL Skills at Home (p. 96) • Tip Sheet 12: Practicing Forgiveness (p. 117) • Tip Sheet 17: My Resiliency Strategies (p. 144) • Tip Sheet 22: Coping With Stress (p. 166) • Worksheet 5: Wheel of Emotion (p.86)
Reframing the Impact of Traumatic Events	• Tip Sheet 13: Rewriting My Story (p. 134) • Tip Sheet 14: Looking Toward the Future (p. 136) • Tip Sheet 15: Talking About Trauma (p. 138) • Worksheet 8: Strength of My Trauma (p. 140)

How does trauma and exposure to ACEs factor into this concern? I see a couple of concerns for the current generations of children: (1) increased use of technology to perpetuate trauma (i.e., cyberbullying), and (2) increased barriers to resiliency development and the subsequent increased negative impact to traumatic events. Both concerns are rooted in the research around technology use and adolescent development. According to the Cyberbullying Research Center, a 2019 survey indicated the prevalence of cyberbullying to be more than 36%. This means that approximately one in three children between the ages of 12 and 17 in the study stated that they had been the victim of cyberbullying in their lifetime. Other respondents (30%) indicated being cyberbullied more than twice in the last 30 days (Patchin, 2019), nearly double similar surveys conducted in 2007. To make matters worse, Twenge et al.'s (2018) research suggests a reduction in social-emotional skills, especially prosocial skills and resiliency, as a result of excessive technology exposure. The reduction in these skills can increase the potential negative impacts of chronic trauma and toxic stress even more.

Fortunately, this situation need not be permanent. Balancing the role of smartphones and other technology along with specific strategies to grow and develop resiliency can help change the outcomes for children. My book *The Caring Child* (Fonseca, 2019) discusses many ways to nurture and develop emotional intelligence (EQ), resilience, and empathy in children. Additional strategies can be found in Tip Sheet 1: Balancing the Negative Impact of Technology.

....

Healing the Heart

Chapter 1 introduced adverse childhood experiences, or ACEs, and how they impact the brain and body throughout the lifetime. Before you continue to Chapter 2, take a moment to note your specific concerns regarding trauma and your children in Part 2 of Worksheet 1.

Heart-Centered Ideas

- ACEs are common.
- ACEs impact the brain and bodies of children and adults, with potential negative health and learning outcomes.
- Our current generations of children may be even more impacted by ACEs.
- Parents and other caring adults can reduce the negative impact of ACEs in a variety of ways.

Tip Sheet 1

Balancing the Negative Impact of Technology

○ Set boundaries for screentime and smartphone use. Aim for 2.5 hours a day or less.
○ Discuss the potential negative impact of technology with children.
○ Teach children how to interact with technology in a positive and productive way.
○ Engage with technology with your children through game playing or discussing movies.
○ Take digital breaks as a family.
○ Establish specific boundaries for when it is okay and not okay to engage in screentime use.

Trauma-Informed Practices: ACEs in the Classroom

The impact of ACEs, chronic trauma, and the resultant stress are not limited to the home environment. In school, the impact is often seen in students' ability to learn, emotional regulation, memory and attention, and behavior. Many of the problem behaviors that students demonstrate can be linked back to exposure to ACEs.

Some of the more typical behaviors seen in students impacted by trauma include (The National Child Traumatic Stress Network, 2018):

- anxiety or worry about safety for self and others,
- preoccupation with concerns of violence,
- poor concentration,
- increases in anger and aggressive behavior,
- changes in the ability to manage emotional responses,
- hyperarousal,
- avoidant behaviors, and
- reexperiencing trauma.

In adolescents, behaviors may also include:
- increased absenteeism,
- drug or alcohol use, and
- increased risky behaviors, including sexual behaviors and impulsivity.

One way to think about the behaviors is through the lens of fight-flight-freeze. Students adversely impacted by trauma often function from an activation of their stress responses. Viewing the behavior through the lens of the stress response is one way to begin to interpret their behaviors. Part II explores the impact of trauma within the learning environment in more detail. For now, understand that trauma and ACEs are far more common than previously understood. Also understand that the impact of exposure to traumatic events affects the whole child and crosses into all environments, including the school.

Fortunately, there are many things educators can do to support students who have been exposed to trauma. It begins with becoming trauma informed across the educational system. Specific information regarding trauma-informed practices within the school setting can be found in Part III.

Healing Actions

- Create a list of any trauma-related concerns you have for you or your children.
- Determine your ACEs score and that of your children.
- If you scored a 4 or greater (or if your children did), consider the impact to health and learning outcomes.
- If needed, seek support through the school, medical, or mental health communities.

Chapter 2
Beyond Your Control

♡

Traumatic childhood experiences are not the only types of experiences that adversely impact both children and adults. Natural disasters and other events beyond a person's control can also result in toxic stress that adversely impact a person's mental and physical functioning. As I mentioned in Chapter 1, trauma occurs within a community context. It is for this reason that impacts to the larger community can have a similar pattern of impact as ACEs.

This chapter examines the acute and potentially chronic trauma that occurs as a result of a variety of experiences, ranging from catastrophes like hurricanes and wildfires, to the impact of poverty and community-based violence, to collective trauma experienced through significant world events like 9/11 and acts of terrorism. Similar to the toxic stress created by adverse childhood experiences, these events have the potential to overwhelm a person's ability to cope to such a degree that the stress responses move from adaptive to unhealthy and toxic. It is at that point that people may experience feelings and behaviors similar to post-traumatic stress disorder, or PTSD. In the developing minds and bodies of children, this can be particularly impactful.

Natural Disasters

2018 was one of the deadliest forest fire seasons of all time. More than 8.8 million acres were burned across the Unites States, with more than 8,500 homes destroyed in Northern California in just two of the more than 58,000 total fires that year (Insurance Information Institute, n.d.). In addition to the increase in devastating fires, hurricanes and other major storms resulting in significant flooding have impacted homeowners and businesses in record numbers. There is no denying that major natural and manmade disasters can have a lasting impact on communities.

Children and families are displaced from their homes, personal items are lost and need to be replaced, places of employment may be destroyed resulting in lost wages and jobs—all of these potential outcomes have the capacity to traumatize adults and children.

Typically, the type of trauma caused by one-time disasters is referred to as acute trauma. Although the impact may be severe, it is generally short-lived. Most people are able to demonstrate incredible resilience and rise above the trauma after the disaster has passed.

This is not always the case, however. Sometimes, the acute trauma is compounded as disasters repeat or additional stressors (i.e., financial and medical) cause a family's recovery to stall, retraumatizing the family. As the incidents begin to add up, acute trauma moves to chronic trauma, often with a similar impact to the trauma experienced with ACEs.

The devastating Camp Fire in Paradise, CA, demonstrates the cascading impact of a natural disaster and the potential for chronic trauma. This fire is considered the deadliest fire in recent California history, destroying more than 19,000 structures in the Northern California town, including more than 13,000 homes. Six months after the event, more than 1,000 people were still looking for housing (Insurance Information Institute, n.d.). The fire itself caused acute trauma. The resultant homelessness crisis increased the trauma to chronic trauma for a number of families. With more than 600 businesses also destroyed in the fire, joblessness and poverty also increased, adding to the trauma already being experienced within that community. As the events piled up, the stress response increased. It is reasonable to assume that, for many, the stress responses became toxic, resulting in the potential for many negative outcomes, especially for children.

Poverty

Poverty can devastate communities, increasing incidents of ACEs. More than one in five children live in a state of poverty. The negative outcomes of families living in poverty are well established, increasing the likelihood of ACEs significantly. Children living in poverty have significant negative impacts in the neurobiological and mental health domains, similar to the impact of ACEs. The link is so significant, in fact, that many researchers consider poverty to be an adverse experience in and of itself (Hughes & Tucker, 2018).

For many families that live in poverty, the services designed to help support them can also become the barrier to economic health, making it difficult for families to move out of poverty. This can result in continued exposure to trauma, increased toxic stress, and increased negative outcomes. As said many times already, trauma happens within a context. In the case of poverty, the community of poverty often retraumatizes itself and perpetuates the trauma, resulting in historical or generational trauma and families struggling to get out of the poverty cycle.

In order to reduce the negative impact of trauma, states should adopt policies that are trauma-informed, providing safety, understanding, support, and self-determination for those impacted.

Community Violence

Community violence refers to exposure to intentional acts of interpersonal violence committed in public areas by nonrelatives. Bullying, public shootings, and acts of terrorism are all examples of community violence. Violence perpetrated by community institutions—including religious organizations, safety personnel (e.g., police officers), and educators—can all be included in this type of traumatic experience. Typically, community violence occurs without warning. And, unlike natural disasters, the intent of the event is to harm others. For these reasons, community violence can often result in particularly heightened traumatic responses, creating a heightened sense of fear and overwhelm.

Children are impacted by community violence when they witness the violent acts and when they are a victim to the events. The result is similar to that of acute and chronic trauma, and can often lead to toxic levels of stress and long-term negative outcomes, depending on the severity, intensity, and duration of the traumatic event.

As with other forms of trauma, the impact to individuals varies greatly. You cannot assume that each person will react negatively to trauma. Many times, humans demonstrate incredible resilience. However, as the events accumulate and the stress moves from adaptive to maladaptive, and perhaps even to toxic, the capacity of anyone to overcome the negative impact of trauma becomes compromised. When that could happen is highly individualized. Recognize that it can happen, and more importantly, that there are things you can do to help improve any of the negative outcomes. Worksheet 2: Potentially Traumatizing Events allows space for you to list the events that may cause overwhelm and trauma for you and your children.

··

Childhood Traumatic Grief

Another type of traumatic experience occurs when a child experiences the death of a loved one. This death can be sudden and unexpected—as in the case of a medical emergency, car accident, or act of violence—or expected, as with a long-term illness. Regardless of the reason, death is difficult to process. Children will go through a grief process. This process often includes some regression of behaviors, like bed-wetting and thumb sucking in young children. It may also include irritable behaviors, sadness, sleep and eating problems, and poor school performance.

In a typical grief process, a child may cope with the loss in painful ways that include anger, guilt, confusion, and sadness. But the child will

Worksheet 2
Potentially Traumatizing Events

Directions: List different events that have overwhelmed you or your child's coping ability. List the impact you or your child felt as a result of those events.

Event Type	Event Description	Impact
What Type of Event Was It?	What Specifically Occurred?	What Happened as a Result of the Experience?
ACEs		
Poverty		
Natural Disasters		

Event Type	Event Description	Impact
Medical Emergencies and Long-Term Illness		
Community Violence		
Traumatic Death		
Other:		
Other:		

be able to accept the realities and permanence of death. They will be able to adjust to the changes that death may bring in their life.

Sometimes, a child isn't able to process the loss of a loved one. They are unable to accept the death and deal with the resultant changes. They block any happy memories of the person who has died, remembering only the extreme pain and torment of the death itself. Traumatizing images and memories of the death circle their thoughts, sometimes resulting in numbing and avoidant behaviors, increased mental health challenges, and other negative outcomes (The National Child Traumatic Stress Network, n.d.-b).

For these children, the death itself is a traumatic trigger. Grief of the loss can result in disruption to their development, poor emotional regulation, and a breakdown in the ability to move through the grief processes. Without support, the trauma of the death can result in similar negative outcomes to other forms of trauma. Tip Sheet 2: Supporting Children Who Experience Loss provides some strategies for intervening in cases of traumatic grief. Remember to enlist the help of mental health professional as needed to ensure appropriate bereavement after a significant loss.

··

Trauma-Informed Practices:
The Aftermath of a School Shooting

On November 14, 2019, Saugus High School in California became the latest school to be impacted by a school shooting. A student shot a pistol at five classmates, killing two, and then killed himself. The day after the incident, a friend and educator in that district spoke with me about her concerns. The fear in her voice was palpable. But not only fear. Also anger. Rage. She was mad that this had happened, again. She was frustrated that nothing had changed, that students were still coming to school and losing their lives. It was overwhelming to her, and with good reason. By December 8, 2019, there had been more than 390 mass shootings in the United States in 2019. Saugus was the 44th school shooting in 2019 (Gun Violence Archive, 2019).

Tip Sheet 2

Supporting Children Who Experience Loss

- Be willing to answer questions or talk about the loss.
- Help children understand the normal grief processes, including the emotional and behavioral regulation difficulties that may occur.
- Avoid forcing a discussion of loss before the child is ready.
- Create a supportive environment at home and at school.
- Balance expectations with flexibility when making demands on the child.
- If you have also experienced the loss, be sure to manage your emotions and process fully.
- Enlist help from school and mental health resources as needed to help process through the grief.

The terrifying fact is that school shootings have become all too common. Schools have added lockdown and active shooter drills to the earthquake and fire drill rotation. Educators wrestle with issues of allowing adults to carry weapons for protection. Students wonder about safety as they walk through their schools. Every day, conversations are held regarding school safety and ensuring that students can come to school and learn without fear of being in a mass shooting.

After the shooting at Saugus, the district closed the schools for the rest of the week and grief counselors were provided to any who needed assistance. Saugus High School remained closed until after the Thanksgiving break. As my friend went back to school after the event, she wondered what to do to help her students, how to deal with the many questions and fear she assumed would be on their minds given the close community within the district. We talked at length about her feelings, how to help students, and what she could do.

"I don't see how the curriculum matters right now. I want to be able to support their questions, first. Talk about real things, you know?" "I get it," I said. And I did. It's hard to know exactly what to do after a major tragedy.

The truth is that many of the students may be afraid. They will be seeking safety and normalcy. They will need to know they are safe. I spoke with my friend about ways to build safety and predictability at school. We discussed the need to return things to normal without ignoring the truth of what people may be experiencing. We discussed managing emotions—hers and her students'.

My friend returned to school and normalcy—a new normal, for certain. But normalcy, all the same. Her students did come to her and talk about their feelings. They collectively talked about grief, loss, and healing. She let her students guide the conversations. She tied things back into the curriculum gently. Most of all, she and the students supported each other.

Tip Sheet 3: Supporting Students After a Mass Shooting provides many strategies for managing adult and student distress and supporting the educational environment after a mass shooting. Note that the best response to school shootings is to be as proactive as possible—not in terms of active shooter drills, but by developing and maintaining a positive school climate. It won't solve every problem. But creating an environment in which all students can flourish and support is provided—in academics and mental health—for those who need it is one of the best ways to reduce the risk for school shootings to occur.

Healing the Heart

Chapter 2 broadened the conversation about trauma to include the impact of natural disasters, poverty, and community violence on children. Specific focus was given to the effects of school shootings and traumatic grief.

Heart-Centered Ideas

- Trauma reactions can be caused by natural disasters, community acts of violence, and world events.
- Acute trauma can turn into chronic trauma when traumatic events repeat or accumulate.

Tip Sheet 3

Supporting Students After a Mass Shooting

- o Keep routines as normal as possible, as soon as possible.
- o Be honest and share information with students as developmentally appropriate.
- o Listen to students' fears and concerns.
- o Reassure students that although there are bad people who do bad things, the world is generally a safe place.
- o If you are struggling with the experience, deal with your own emotional needs first.
- o Rebuild and reaffirm attachments and positive relationships in the educational environment.
- o Train school personnel in mental health first aid techniques before a crisis occurs.

- Poverty can function like ACEs and have a similar long-term impact.
- There are specific strategies for dealing with loss and stress that can increase resilience and improve the outcome for people who experience significant levels of trauma.

Healing Actions

- List the trauma-impacting events you and your children may have experienced.
- Add to the previous list of trauma-related concerns, if needed.
- Begin to think about how stress manifests in you and your children.

Chapter 3
How Humans Respond to Stress

$\heartsuit$

The human body has a built-in alarm system, alerting you to danger and equipping you with everything necessary to ensure survival—your stress response system. At its most adaptive, your stress system prepares you to meet the challenge of an adverse experience and protects both the body and mind from undue harm created by the event. Unfortunately, a stress response can be pushed beyond its limits and fail. This occurs most frequently in moments of extreme trauma or after repeated exposure to adverse experience. At these times, your stress response system moves from adaptive to unhealthy. Your thinking can become rigid, and your mind and body prepare to survive whatever you are experiencing, no matter the cost. This chapter explores all of the aspects of the stress response, and how stress moves from adaptive to unhealthy.

The Gift of Stress

Stress—you can't escape it. It's the feeling of excitement you get when you are about to speak in front of a crowd. Or the adrenaline rush you experience just before the big game. Or the nervousness you sense when you reach out to a friend to go with you to the doctor to get the answers you don't really want. All of these occasions activate your internal alarm system that urges you into some sort of action.

Far from a negative thing, your adaptive stress response is designed to keep you safe, motivate you into action, let you know when to seek community and comfort, and help you learn from your experiences to better prepare you for what life delivers in the future. Your stress response system is the reason you are able to survive and flourish. Except when it isn't.

More on that in a moment. For now, I want you to fully understand how the body responds to stressful events. It starts with a triggering event, something that sets off the brain's internal alarm system. Typically, this is something external, like an alarm going off or an important meeting at work. Internal events—things like remembering an argument or thinking about someone you've lost—can also trigger your stress response. Once your internal alarm system is ignited, your fight-flight-freeze response kicks in.

To understand how this works, you need to have a general understanding of your brain's functioning. I'm oversimplifying it a bit, but I just need you to understand the basics. The brain has three main areas: (1) the hindbrain, often called the "downstairs" brain; (2) the midbrain; and (3) the forebrain, often called the "upstairs" brain. The hindbrain handles basic life functions, like eating and breathing. The forebrain generally handles complex thinking, language, logic, and reasoning. The midbrain functions like a relay station between the hind- and forebrains. Within this region lives memory, emotional regulation, and threat perception. One way to think of this is as follows: Your forebrain gives you your logical voice, your midbrain provides your emotional voice, and your hindbrain is your survival voice.

When the stress response is at optimal functioning, there are high levels of integration in the brain. Lateral and vertical communication are efficiently occurring, and the brain is able to adapt to the various stressors that occur. Consider the following example: Your alarm goes off in the morning, pulling you from a deep sleep. Immediately, the sound activates your internal stress response. Your heartbeat and adrenaline activate, pulling you from your sleep. You sit up, ready to respond to any present danger. Using the rational thinking of your forebrain, you look around and assess the situation. You realize that it is just your alarm waking you for the day. You take a breath and turn off the alarm, recognizing that there is no danger present. Your forebrain sends the all-clear signal throughout the rest of your brain, and you begin to calm. Your breathing slows, your heartbeat calms, and within moments, you have returned to a calm state.

This is a positive and adaptive stress response. I often refer to this as a Stage 1 response. It is your short-acting, immediate fight-flight-freeze response you often think of when you think about stress. This part of your stress response fires quickly and is meant to be short, often lasting for seconds—just long enough to get you out of danger and determine if the threat is over. This is the normal stress response many people exhibit when triggered by everyday stressors, including new situations, meeting new people, public speaking, and the like.

But what happens when the triggering threat continues, when the event is something bigger than a blaring alarm clock? What happens when the stressor is the loss of a family member, or a natural disaster, or a medical emergency?

When you are faced with more significant stressful or traumatizing events that last for a longer period of time, additional aspects of your stress response are activated. I call this a Stage 2 response. In this case, oxytocin is added to your adrenaline response, compelling you to reach out to others for help and/or aid those in need. Additionally, your brain begins to conserve your body's energy stores in order to preserve your survival. Your forebrain begins to form ways to ameliorate the threat and survive (Fonseca, 2018).

This stage can result in some negative impacts to your overall functioning, including stress-related negative impacts to your health and increased signs of anxiety. If the threat resolves, calming the activation of the stress cycle, and you are able to support others or be supported by others, especially your loved ones, the potential negative outcomes are buffered. Additional oxytocin is produced, protecting and healing your organs from the harmful effects of cortisol. Your brain learns that it can trust others to help during a crisis, and your stress response system is bolstered (McGonigal, 2015).

However, when the threat lingers and you do not have support from loved ones, the negative impact of this stage or your stress response can begin to wear down the integration of your brain's processes, resulting in more negative outcomes. This is what you often hear about stress—the potential harmful effects of stress to the heart and other organs, as well as the increase in anxiety and other mental health concerns related to stress.

When Stress Hurts

Sometimes, the stressful and/or traumatizing event is strong, prolonged, or frequent. When this occurs, your stress response system enters what I call Stage 3—toxic stress. This occurs in many cases of trauma, especially chronic trauma. Events like ACEs, community violence, and poverty will often overtax your stress response system, creating a toxic stress response.

In this stage, the brain works toward survival at all costs. Energy is conserved to a large degree. This means that the brain shows preference for previously learned behaviors that resulted in your survival, no matter how maladaptive those behaviors may be. If your child ran from the room screaming in response to a traumatic event in the past, resulting in surviving that experience, they may run from a classroom when similarly triggered, even though they have learned a different behavioral response. This is because it takes less energy to use a habituated response pattern than activate new learning (Fonseca, 2018).

In addition to preserving energy through the use of previous behavioral patterns, the brain will lock down all new learning. The brain and body work together to resist change and maintain the status quo. In this state, children are unable to learn, the body's healing mechanism is less efficient, and the hindbrain makes most decisions. Everything is about survival in the short run.

The negative outcomes are exacerbated the longer and more frequently the triggering events occur. Lack of support of caring adults can disrupt brain and body development in children and intensify negative outcomes for both children and adults (St. Andrews, 2013).

This is the brain impacted by toxic levels of stress.

The Impact of Toxic Stress

The past two chapters have discussed the types of traumatic events children and adults may experience, as well as the brain's stress response to normal, everyday stressors and traumatic events. You need to understand how the stress response system moves to toxic and how traumatic events fit into that dynamic. As children experience various types of adverse experiences, they experience trauma. Table 3 defines and describes the most common types of trauma. As different traumatic events occur, a child may move from acute trauma to chronic trauma and eventually into complex trauma. When this occurs, the stress response system moves from adaptive to toxic, and the major negative impacts described earlier often occur.

Note that anyone can experience toxic levels of stress from a single traumatic event. Secondary or vicarious trauma can overwhelm one's coping mechanisms, resulting in toxic levels of stress, as can historical or intergenerational trauma. Recognizing the impact of toxic stress is the key to supporting children and adults impacted by trauma.

As mentioned earlier, toxic stress impacts all areas of functioning. Part II looks in depth at the impact to the developing brains and bodies of children. For now, Table 4 provides a quick reference to the major symptoms of toxic stress you may see in cognitive, physical, emotional, and social-behavioral domains (Fonseca, 2018; St. Andrews, 2013).

....

Trauma as a Mental Health Condition

For some children and adults impacted by ACEs and other traumatic experiences, the toxic stress created by the events causes a level of mental health impairment that adversely impacts daily functioning. When this happens, a variety of mental health conditions may occur. For many years, the diagnoses related to toxic stress were predominately consid-

Table 3

A Continuum of Trauma

Type of Trauma	Definition of Trauma
Acute Trauma	A single, traumatic event.
Chronic Trauma	Multiple and/or prolonged exposure to traumatic events.
Complex Developmental Trauma	Children's experience of multiple traumatic events (chronic trauma) and the cumulative impact the exposure has on overall development.
Toxic Stress	Maladaptive stress response due to prolonged exposure to adverse experiences that overwhelm a person's ability to cope.
Vicarious Trauma	The impact to cognitive thinking as a result of exposure to the trauma of others.
Secondary Stress Response	A maladaptive stress response similar to toxic stress that results from exposure to the trauma of others (real and imagined).
Compassion Fatigue	The cumulative physical, emotional, and psychological effects of exposure to traumatic stories or events when working in a helping capacity.
Historical or Generational Trauma	Collective, large-scale trauma that results from multiple and/or significant oppressions over time within societies (i.e., genocide, slavery, internment).

ered anxiety disorders. However, in the latest edition of the *Diagnostic and Statistical Manual of Mental Disorders* (DSM-V; American Psychiatric Association, 2013), a greater recognition of the significant impact of toxic stress on multiple areas of functioning resulted in a new chapter called "Trauma and Stressor-Related Disorders." Although the DSM-V failed to include developmental trauma disorder (DTD), despite research indicating the significance of the disorder (van der Kolk, 2014), the chapter did specify many disorders associated with trauma and toxic stress.

The primary disorder identified in the new chapter is PTSD, which focuses on individuals who have directly experienced or witnessed traumatic events. The chapter does not address the cumulative impact of chronic or complex trauma, nor does it address intergenerational or historic trauma (van der Kolk, 2005). Despite the limitations of the disorder, PTSD is the most commonly used diagnosis in addressing trauma-related

Table 4

Symptoms of Toxic Stress

Domain	Symptoms
Cognitive	• Distorted or intrusive thinking • Impaired attention and concentration • Disruptions to executive functioning • Nightmares • Impaired memory
Emotional	• Increased fears • Increased sadness and depression-like feelings • Increased worry and anxious-like feelings • Helplessness • Emotional intensity and/or emotional numbing
Social/ Behavioral	• Increased aggression and violence • School impairment or refusal • Poor relationship skills • Poor social skills • Increased risky behaviors • Increased tantrum • Decreased frustration tolerance

mental health conditions. Changes to the PTSD criteria for the DSM-V included a broadening of the diagnosis for the preschool subtype and the addition of a dissociative subtype. These changes begin to take into consideration current trauma-related research, but they still fail to recognize the significant impact of toxic stress.

As research continues into the appropriateness of the inclusion of DTD, more mental health diagnostic options may become available to mental health providers when treating the significant impact of toxic stress and trauma. Early discussion of DTD includes the following four areas of impact (Friedman, n.d.):

- **impaired arousal regulation:** difficulties processing and regulating extreme emotions, disturbances in multiple areas of daily functioning and sensory regulation, impaired emotional vocabulary, and dissociation of emotional states.
- **impaired cognitive regulation and coping strategies:** hyperarousal of threat perception, willingness to take extreme risks,

habitual self-harm, maladaptive self-calming strategies, and inability to maintain goal-directed behaviors.

- **impaired interpersonal processes:** intense preoccupation with the safety of others, poor self-concept, inappropriate sexual behaviors, impaired empathy regulation, and inability to form and maintain appropriate relationships or boundaries.
- **impaired function in life:** difficulties maintaining adequate school or work performance, violent behavior with others, and poor maintenance of physical health.

As I review the impacts listed here, each one connects to the specific impacts toxic stress has on the developing brains and bodies of children. Part II goes into more depth in each of these areas of impact, and Part III provides ways to intercede and support children impacted by trauma.

Trauma-Informed Practices: Toxic Stress in the Classroom

The impact of toxic stress is not limited to the home environment or the internal states of individuals. Toxic stress can also result in behaviors that impact the classroom environment. Consider the intense fight-flight-freeze behavior that occurs with a stress response. When the response is adaptive, students can regulate the behavior quickly once the threat is neutralized. But with toxic stress, the threat never lessens. Fight becomes a desperate need to control one's environment in order to best survive. Flight becomes an all-consuming need to escape, physically or emotionally. Freeze becomes an attempt to hide. As students demonstrate the toxic versions of their stress responses, the behaviors are easily mislabeled as noncompliant, combative, uncooperative, difficult, and unmotivated (Fonseca, 2018; St. Andrews, 2013).

Tip Sheet 4

Toxic Stress Comes to School

Students experiencing toxic stress may:

- Struggle with sequencing skills.
- Struggle with verbal processes.
- Be limited in problem-solving skills.
- Struggle with cause-and-effect relationships.
- Struggle with perspective taking.
- Struggle with self-regulation.
- Struggle with empathy and compassion.
- Demonstrate poor impulse control.
- Demonstrate weak or underdeveloped prosocial skills.
- Demonstrate weak executive functioning skills.
- Struggle to take academic risks.
- Demonstrate poor relationship skills.
- Demonstrate low academic engagement.
- Demonstrate low motivation.

These definitions do not explain the true feelings inside. Youth exposed to chronic trauma often do anything to survive. They actively dissociate from their feelings and memories, push away from relationships with adults and peers, and abandon their sense of trust and safety. All of this happens as a way to protect themselves: to survive.

As discussed earlier in the chapter, toxic stress results in a reduction of energy as the brain shuts down in favor of survival. This leaves little available mental energy for many of the necessary learning functions in school, including concentration, memory, attention, interpersonal skills, and emotional and behavioral regulation (Fonseca, 2018). Tip Sheet 4: Toxic Stress Comes to School lists several of the most common classroom behaviors. Becoming trauma-informed begins with understanding all of the ways trauma and toxic stress may appear in the classroom.

Healing the Heart

Chapter 3 focused on the impact of trauma on our ability to respond to stress. Specific attention was given to complex trauma and toxic stress and their impact on physical and psychological health.

Heart-Centered Ideas

- The human stress response is typically adaptive and assists our coping mechanisms.
- The stress response moves from adaptive to maladaptive and toxic with increased environmental, physical, and psychological demands.
- Increases in frequency or intensity of trauma can shift the stress response from adaptive to toxic.
- Toxic levels of stress adversely impact all aspects of human functioning.

Healing Actions

- Develop a stress response menu and coping menu for you and your children. See Tip Sheet 5: My Stress Response Menu.
- Determine what shifts, if any, are needed to improve your stress response.

Tip Sheet 5

My Stress Response Menu

Try one of these strategies to help you manage your stress response.

- **Mindfulness Practices:** Develop daily mindfulness practices, including breathing exercises, meditation, mindful exercise, or other mindfulness tasks.
- **Breathing Colors:** Take several deep breaths. On the inhalation, picture your favorite color. On the exhalation, imagine a dirty color. This is the color of the stress in your body. Continue slow, steady breathing until the color you inhale matches the color you exhale.
- **Mini Vacations:** Take a break whenever you are overwhelmed with mental vacations. Pick your vacation spot. Imagine everything about that place—how things look, how they feel, how they smell. The more vivid, the better. Immerse yourself in the vacation for 5 or 6 minutes.
- **Tense and Release:** Systematically tense and relax your major muscle groups, one by one, incorporating deep breathing and mindfulness into the actions.

Note. Adapted from *Emotional Intensity in Gifted Students: Helping Kids Cope With Explosive Feelings* (2nd ed., p. 84), by C. Fonseca, 2016, Prufrock Press. Copyright 2016 by Prufrock Press. Adapted with permission.

Chapter 4
Through My Eyes

Conversations With a Trauma-Impacted Adult—*Tina's Story*

♡

In September, 2017, I traveled to Houston, TX, for a speaking engagement. It was about 4 weeks after Hurricane Harvey had hit. The ground was still waterlogged. The air continued to have a slight odor of mold and decay. As I got into my rental car, I noticed the detour and construction signs throughout the city and suburbs. It was surreal. I knew right then that I wanted to talk to people about the experience of living through Harvey. I wanted to hear their stories and witness the recovery efforts.

For the next 2 days, I spoke to anyone who was willing to talk with me. The front desk personnel and housekeeping staff at the Courtyard, the teachers who came to hear me speak, the shuttle driver who drove me from the car rental building to the airport departure building—everyone shared their personal stories of loss and triumph.

I visited Houston again in November. Recovery was fully underway. People were somewhat happier. I spoke with groups about trauma and healing after major events like Harvey. I gathered even more stories about loss, rebuilding, and the resiliency of the human spirit.

I decided to focus this conversation on a particularly poignant story I heard during that first visit a month after the hurricane had hit. I met Tina (not her real name) at the airport in Houston, making my way from the busy car rental building back to the airport to catch a flight home.

Tina told me that she and her family lost nearly everything in the floods that followed Harvey. As I asked her about her story, I was struck by her optimism and hope in the face of devastating loss. The following is a recount of that conversation:

♡ ♡ ♡

"How are you doing?" I asked of the person seated behind the wheel of the empty shuttle bus. She was a large woman with ebony skin and eyes that seemed like they could reach into my soul.

She blinked her eyes and quietly said, "Fine," before pulling onto the road.

"No, really," I continued to say, "how are you?"

The woman—Tina, she would tell me later—peered into the mirrors and locked her gaze with mine. "To tell you the truth," she said, "things have been tough."

"I'm sure they have. I have been talking to people about their experiences. I'd love to hear your story."

"I'm sure it's no different than most people's," she began. "The rain came and poured with such ferocity I thought it would never end. We fared better than most, I think. My family and me. We had someplace to go. That wasn't true for a lot of people."

"Were you in your house when the storm hit?" I asked.

"No, like I said, we had someplace to go. We took the warnings seriously and left as soon as they told us to. We went to my parents'—me, my husband, and our three children. They live a few hours away. It rained there, but it didn't flood."

"Did you have friends who stayed and rode out the storm?"

"Yep. Not all of them survived, either. Some just left too late and got swept away by the water. Some hunkered down, climbing up to the roof when the waters rose. Some were rescued. It was a horrible time. But, like I said, we were lucky. We got out."

"And when you got back to your house? What had happened?"

"We haven't gone back, really." Tina's eyes welled. "Our house was a total loss. We have nothing left." She paused for a moment before continuing her story. "That's not totally true. We have our important papers, our insurance and stuff. And we have each other. That's all that really matters. We can replace the rest. It's hard, though. Every time it rains I get worried. So do the kids. You can see it in their eyes. They ask if Grandpa's house is going to be okay or if we're going to have to leave again."

"That must be hard," I said.

"It is. I just remind them that we're together and we're okay."

"Did you have flood insurance?" I asked out of curiosity.

"Yeah. But getting things settled is tough. The insurance adjuster wants receipts. I keep trying to explain that any receipts we had washed away with the flood. You'd think they'd know that, right? They ask anyway. And every time they ask, I feel like I'm back in the hurricane all over again."

I paused for a bit to allow Tina a moment. "What do you think about now? Recovery? Moving forward?" I asked.

"Those things, sure. Mostly I count my blessings."

Her answer surprised me. "Really? That's surprising."

"It's true. I have a job. Many of my friends had their businesses destroyed. They have no way to provide for their families. Not me. I still have this job. And even though the insurance red tape is hard, at least we had insurance. Not everyone does. And look around— Houston is resilient. We are starting to rebuild. People still come in and out of our little town for business just like you, right?"

"Right," I said with a smile. "Are your children as optimistic as you?"

"Well, you know kids. It is a bit harder. They just see everything they lost. The other day I made them sit in front of the television and watch the reports coming out of Puerto Rico about Maria last week. Now that was a storm. Look at the loss those people are dealing with right now. The entire island looks destroyed. We have it bad. They have it so much worse. I want my children to see the blessings, not just the devastation they feel."

"And how did your children respond?"

"Hurricanes definitely scare them now, so there was a little bit of fear. Mostly, though, they understood what I was saying and [that I] wanted to help them. We decided we would do what we could to help the people there, too."

"That is amazing. I don't know too many people who would be able to do that."

"It's important to count your blessings, no matter how hard that is. I want my children to know that no matter how bleak things seem, there is always something to be thankful for . . . always."

My conversation with Tina ended with a hug as I hopped off the shuttle to catch my flight. I was left with thoughts of her and her resilient spirit. She was a survivor. More, she and her family would thrive because of her optimism and gratitude in the face of such loss. And perhaps this is the best lesson of all—traumatic events don't need to define you in negative ways. Yes, they leave their mark. And yes, there are scars that remain after horrific events. But you can overcome; you can choose to look at life through the lens of optimism and gratitude. And when you can find that spirit, you can bounce back, survive and thrive, no matter how significant the loss.

Part II

Toxic Stress and the Developing Brain

The negative impact of trauma on the developing bodies and brains of children is primarily related to the effect of toxic stress. More than merely maladaptive, toxic levels of stress can disrupt healthy development of the brain, impacting white matter and grey matter development. As communication between various processing components of the brain is disrupted, so, too, are how thoughts and feelings influence behavior.

This section explores all aspects of our body's stress response, from adaptive to maladaptive to toxic. Furthermore, Part II investigates the connection between the disruption of brain functioning and our emotions and behaviors. Finally, the section takes a look at specific diverse populations through a trauma-impacted lens.

In addition to the impact of toxic stress on all aspects of human functioning, the chapters in this section begin to offer guidance as you start to move from understanding to action.

The section ends with the story of a teen's trauma related to being gifted and transgender. Through his story, you see what can happen when one lives within the margins of general society, as well as the impact of trauma on emotionally intense people. The story is one of courage and resilience in the face of ignorance and hate.

Chapter 5
Trauma and the Brain

$\heartsuit$

Rigid thinking, poor generalization and integration of social-emotional skills, fractured relationships, and a heightened threat awareness—this is the brain on trauma. Everything is geared toward survival. This is helpful when in the middle of an actual, life-threatening event. It is less useful when this response continues well beyond the event.

Children who are impacted by repeated, or complex, trauma experience high levels of toxic stress that throw their brains and bodies into a fixed state of arousal and stress. This chapter examines the impact of the constant stress arousal on the brain and the body, providing strategies to help minimize the determinantal impact and move the body's stress response from toxic to adaptive.

Toxic Stress and the Brain

Chapter 3 discussed toxic stress and how your stress response system moves from adaptive to maladaptive to toxic. I spoke about how rigid the brain becomes, the inability of the forebrain to activate fully, and the ways the midbrain and hindbrain overcompensate. To fully understand this dynamic and the full impact of toxic stress on cognitive processes, especially within the developing brain of a child, it is helpful to know how the brain develops throughout childhood more fully. As with my discussion of brain functioning in Chapter 3, this is a somewhat simplistic explanation.

Brain development occurs in two main ways—vertically and laterally. Before birth, the majority of brain development occurs in the brain stem. From 0–2, the cerebellum, within the hindbrain, is the focus of development, with significant physiological movement developing at a healthy rate. During the toddler years, considerable progress typically occurs within the limbic system. This region of the brain regulates emotion and manages threat perception, among other things. As children enter early childhood (ages 3–6), the development of the cortex expands, and more rational judgment begins to develop (Australian Childhood Foundation, 2018).

Laterally, development shifts from the right hemisphere to the left hemisphere and back during the same time frame. The brain begins to integrate processes more fully during mid-childhood (ages 8–9). This integration is what helps to mature emotional intelligence skills and resilience (Thatcher et al., 1987).

The brain's primary function in any human being is to ensure survival. This is accomplished through the integration of sensory input that comes in through all of life's experiences. As different regions of the brain are activated from experience, the brain begins to learn which kinds of events are threatening and which activities are not. You begin to learn how to adapt to the needs and challenges of life, adjusting to the unique physical and relational environments you experience. As your experiences expand, you build new neural pathways throughout your brain. In healthy brain development, more neuropathways lead to greater and more efficient integration. This integration shapes the thoughts-feelings-action chain. Higher integration results in a more adaptive chain, increased emotional intelligence development, and greater resilience (Fonseca, 2019).

When traumatic events cause toxic levels of stress, disruption to both lateral and vertical development can occur. The communication between the various processing centers in the brain is disrupted, resulting in reduced or fractured integration. Healthy neuropathways deteriorate or distort. Integration decreases. Weakened or delayed development of cognitive and emotional processes occurs, and resilience diminishes, making you more vulnerable to the harmful impact of toxic stress. A vicious cycle begins.

If the traumatic events repeatedly happened during childhood, primary to the development of healthy brain integration, the impact can be even greater and significantly impact the development of the whole child. Poor emotional regulation, weak adaptive skills, fractured memories, inconsistent attention, and learning difficulties are all typical in a child who has been negatively impacted by complex developmental trauma and toxic stress (van der Kolk, 2014; Yates, 2007). Poor neural communication and the resultant integration problems lead to disruption of the thinking-feeling-behavior chain, disrupting the development of both emotional intelligence and resilience.

How Trauma Impacts the Body

The impact of complex trauma is not limited to the functioning of the brain. The body is also significantly impacted. Fight-flight-freeze, the major actions of the stress response system, affects the body in a variety of ways. Digestion, reproduction, and other bodily functions slow as the body gears up to manage the impending threat. Attention narrows. Cortisol can narrow the coronary arteries while also increasing blood flow, causing the potential for blockages and damage to the heart. This is part of the reason doctors warn against experiencing too much stress. When the stress response is limited to Stage 1, these bodily actions are short-lived. Even in the second stage of a stress response, the body protects itself through the activation of oxytocin. This stress hormone protects the heart from the adverse effects of cortisol during stress activation.

Toxic stress breaks down oxytocin activation and utilization, and prolongs the exposure to harmful effects of stress. In children, this impact can be magnified, setting up a foundation of disease consistent with the findings of the ACE study (Felitti et al., 1998). As mentioned earlier, complex developmental trauma and the corresponding toxic stress result in the disruption of emotional and cognitive processes. This disruption often manifests in differences in the thinking-feeling-behavior chain in children.

For more children impacted by complex trauma, their brain is hypersensitive to threat. And with good reason. For a child, the best chance of survival is to be vigilant. During periods of stress, this means being on the constant lookout for danger. Change—from the most basic to the most significant—is considered highly threatening and something to be avoided (Gunnar & Quevedo, 2007). Sensory information is frequently misinterpreted as a threat, and behaviors often follow suit.

As the body becomes more and more impacted by trauma and toxic levels of stress, children may look for ways to alleviate the stress. Addictive behaviors, including drug use and engagement in risky behaviors, are common ways to attempt to relieve stress. Dissociation from the body can also occur. In interviews, sexual abuse survivors often talk about disconnecting from their bodies. One student I worked with would describe it as "living outside of her body." She spoke of not feeling things in her body the way her friends did. She felt things too intensely in some moments, and not at all in others. She could cut herself off from her physical feelings and disassociate easily. When she did invite physical contact, like a hug from a friend, she stated that the feeling was often "overwhelming and painful." Her brain's lack of integration of sensory information had resulted in incomplete sensory messages. These incomplete messages, then, perpetuated the integration difficulties in her mind. Another vicious cycle begins.

Memory, Trauma, and Toxic Stress

One of the most significant impacts of complex developmental trauma and toxic stress is the way they affect memory. At birth, memory begins as mostly sensory. Information comes into the brain through the five senses and is processed and stored. As experiences occur, the sensory information is internalized and connected to form predictability and safety. For example, if an infant feels discomfort due to soiling their diapers, they will cry. The parent or caregiver comes and changes the diaper, alleviating the distress. This change of events repeats, and the child internalizes the memory. They soon begin to predict that if they cry out due to discomfort, their needs will be attended to each time. In a healthy environment, their needs are met, and the predictability and safety patterns are established through their memory patterns.

As the child's limbic system and cortex develop, memory becomes more complex. As well as sensory information, feelings and specific details about events are stored. A healthy developing brain integrates these parts of memory, coding them to connect when being retrieved. Complete memories that include sensory, emotional, and concrete details about events can be retrieved as single memories. This processing pathway connects with the learning aspects of the stress response cycle, and humans begin to use memory as a way to learn from experiences and anticipate outcomes from new events. The ability to generalize skills across experiences can also occur (Brown et al., 2007).

When traumatic events and toxic stress impact a child, significant disruption occurs to memory pathways and processing. The integration of the different facets of memory deteriorates. No longer do the feelings, sensory stimuli, and concrete details of memory link together. The feelings of events can link to the sensory pieces absent the specific details. Associations become detached. Learning becomes fragments. The generalization of skills is hampered. In this scenario, a child can have a traumatic memory linked to specific sensory cues and feelings, but not remember the exact details of the memory—what explicitly happened or where or when it happened. This is what happens with repressed memories.

I remember one young adult I worked with several years ago. He had been the victim of incest but had repressed the memory for several years. Molested by a drunk family member, he had strong physical and emotional reactions whenever he smelled alcohol. The specific event occurred during a rainstorm, so the sound and smell of rain could also trigger strong negative emotions. Whenever either sensory stimulation occurred, he would get scared and angry, and try to flee the situation. When asked why he felt that way, he only responded with, "I don't know." At that time, he was unable to recall the actual event or link his

Trauma-Informed Practices:
Trauma and Learning

Complex developmental trauma and toxic stress impact more than physiological functioning. There are significant impacts on memory, cognitive processes, and learning. As discussed in Chapter 3, a person's stress response inhibits the activation of the cortex, or "upstairs brain." When something happens to trigger a trauma-impacted child, the "downstairs brain" is ignited, temporal distortion often occurs, and the child functions as though the traumatic event is currently happening (Blodgett & Dorado, n.d.).

In addition to the neurobiological compromise through the negative impact of trauma on the brain and body, emotional reactions are impacted. Chapter 6 details the significant impact of trauma on emotional development and behavior. With learning, the compromised emotional system further strains the brain's ability to take in new knowledge. As the downstairs brain is activated, the capacity to take in new information is limited. Further, change in any way often ignites the threat centers of the brain and is characterized as a threat. As the emotional and behavioral regulation systems continue to struggle, children often dissociate from their thinking skills. The behavior is in charge, and reactions can be volatile (Willis, 2018).

Strains to the memory system can often add to the stressors students feel in school by making learning even more challenging. With compromised and potentially degraded memory, children may struggle to recall information, synthesize learning, and build necessary learning scripts to facilitate future learning. The impact worsens when a child's trauma story is triggered.

Many things within the school setting can trigger trauma-impacted reactions from children. Changes in routine, unpredictable classrooms, confrontation, and sensory overload are all typical triggers for students impacted by complex trauma and toxic stress. Even compliments and positive performance feedback can activate a trauma cycle of behavior if the attention is considered as a threat or makes excessive demands on their cognitive skills.

reaction to that event. It wasn't until several years later, when the memories reintegrated, that he was able to see the connection between the sensory trigger, his emotions, and the actual traumatic event.

As memories lack connectivity in a brain impacted by toxic stress and complex trauma, the memory fragments lose temporal orientation. This means that past and present begin to merge. This can result in retraumatization. Additionally, the fragmented memory becomes a source of stress, adding to the existing stressors on the brain. Memory templates lose their internal meaning, and the capacity to formulate an inner sense of self is compromised. Without a sense of self, internal safety is difficult to establish. Without safety, more stress develops. And again, the vicious cycle continues. All of this—the negative impact on the brain, the body, and memories—can quickly become habituated, rewiring how one responds to stress and stressful situations.

Healing the Heart

Chapter 5 explored the biology of toxic stress and the brain, including the impact of social-emotional learning on resiliency development.

Heart-Centered Ideas

- Toxic stress affects all aspects of neurological processing.
- Due to the connection between brain functioning and bodily health, toxic stress impacts both the brain and the body.
- Memory and learning can be negatively impacted by complex trauma and toxic stress.
- The impact of toxic stress will span a lifetime, although there are ways to improve outcomes at any stage of development.

Healing Actions

- Complete the brain, body, memory, and learning sections of Worksheet 3: The Impact of My Trauma.
- Answer the journal question on Worksheet 4: My Journey Through Trauma related to toxic stress and the brain.

Worksheet 3
The Impact of My Trauma

Directions: Based on your understanding of how complex developmental trauma impacts the development of children, complete the worksheet for each of your children.

Area	Impact *What is the impact to this area of development?*
Brain	
Body	
Memory	

| Area | Impact
What is the impact to this area of development? |
|---|---|
| Learning | |
| Emotions | |
| Behavior | |

Worksheet 4
My Journey Through Trauma

Directions: As you work through *Healing the Heart*, use this worksheet to chronicle your journey to healing and growth.

Chapter 5
1. How has trauma impacted my children's brain, body, and learning?

Chapter 6
1. How has trauma impacted my children's thoughts, feelings, and actions?

Chapter 8

1. Consider the ways your child experiences safety, and answer the following.
   a. How is my child physically safe at home?
   b. How is emotional and psychological safety established for my child?

2. Are there are areas you need to improve in? What can you do to improve the sense of safety your child has at home?

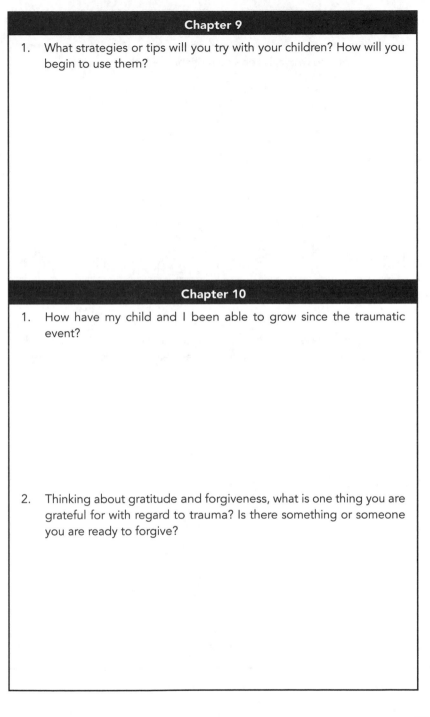

Chapter 9

1. What strategies or tips will you try with your children? How will you begin to use them?

Chapter 10

1. How have my child and I been able to grow since the traumatic event?

2. Thinking about gratitude and forgiveness, what is one thing you are grateful for with regard to trauma? Is there something or someone you are ready to forgive?

Chapter 12

1. Review the progress you have made thus far. What do you notice about you or your children's relationship with the trauma?

2. Determine one to two areas you would like to continue to work through. What is the goal for these areas? How can you achieve your goals?

Chapter 13

1. Take a moment to review the Tip Sheets, as well as the FAQs. What questions do you still have?

2. How will you bring this information to your child's teachers (or education colleagues)?

Chapter 14

1. What are your key takeaways from the exercises and the book? What questions remain?

Chapter 6
Trauma, Emotions, and Behavior

♡

The impact of trauma and toxic stress isn't limited to the brain and body. A person's emotions and behaviors can be significantly altered by exposure to repeated trauma. Chapter 5 examined the ways adverse events alter thinking patterns related to the stories a person might tell themselves in response to the events. As a person's thinking changes, so do their feelings. Changes in one's emotions then result in changes in one's behavior. Often, the first indication of the impact of trauma that parents see is in a child's behavior. Learning to decode the communicative intent of behavior, then, can help you better understand what your child may need and how to best offer support.

Toxic Stress and Emotions

Emotions happen as a result of a person's thinking, and they often initiate specific behaviors. Emotions help children learn to navigate their world. The feelings prepare children for potential events. For example, a child may feel anticipation the night before the first day of school. This anticipation and excitement prepare the child for the emotional rush that may occur the next day, informing the child of the potential need to manage their intense emotions. The anticipation helps the child know what to expect. Just as the feeling of excitement and anticipation prepared the child to meet an emotional challenge, emotions like fear can prepare a child for potential danger. The emotions can ignite the fight-flight response discussed in Chapter 3.

As the brain develops cognitive skills, as known as thinking skills, children's emotional awareness and regulation increase. The thinking skills and emotional processes work in concert to help children begin to understand behavior and internal states. For example, social reactions from others to a child's behavior help the child learn about the consequences of their behavior and their feelings. This leads to increases in social awareness and interpersonally processing skills.

Complex developmental trauma and the ensuing toxic stress disrupt this entire development. Changes in how emotions are processed and stored occur as communication laterally and vertically happens in response to the toxic stress. The integration of language to emotions (lateral communication) is disrupted, and children are unable to develop an adequate emotional vocabulary. Without labels for their feelings, children's ability to communicate information about their feelings, needs, or wants is severely compromised. The ability to develop intra- and interpersonal skills is similarly compromised. Needed skills for the development of compassion and empathy are disrupted (Fonseca, 2019).

With the disruption of vertical communication between the hindbrain, midbrain, and forebrain, children are limited in their ability to utilize complex thinking with emotions. Emotional regulation is compromised, and cognitive skills development halted. Without the benefit of increased thinking skills, behavior inhibition, and attention regulation, feelings can quickly become a source of threat to children. This sets off a chain of increased emotional reactivity, and another vicious cycle begins.

With impaired social awareness due to the impact of toxic stress on emotional processing and storage, the typical social learning pattern is disrupted. Behavior responses from others appear unpredictable, increasing emotional dysregulation. This often results in distrust by trauma-impacted children of the relational environment. The deficits in emotional literacy and poor emotional communication skills often result in children distrusting their own feelings. The disrupted emotional development and poor environmental perception can result in behavior reactions that lack any awareness. Trauma-impacted children often lack an internal barometer for their feelings, making it challenging to regulate emotional responses. With the lack of trust for both the internal and external worlds, children in this situation often close themselves off to the world completely (Australian Childhood Foundation, 2018).

Behavior as Communication

All human behavior serves a specific function. Generally, that function is to get something (i.e., attention, something tangible, or social status) or escape something (i.e., something unpleasant, punishment, blame). Behavior can occur in response to sensory stimuli, as a person may try to get more or less of a particular sensory input. In this way, behavior works as a form of communication, asserting a person's needs and wants. But behavior doesn't occur in isolation. It is the end of a specific change of activity that starts with thoughts, moves into emotions, and ends with a specific action (or, in some cases, inaction). In this way, the behavior is the window to a person's thoughts and feelings. To understand the thoughts and feelings, however, one must first understand behavior.

Decoding behavior begins with understanding the underlying function the behavior serves. For example, if I am yawning, you may assume that I am tired. The behavior of yawning is often a physical response to being understimulated or tired. But yawning doesn't only mean that I need to sleep. Maybe I am yawning because I was holding my breath during a test due to anxiety. The yawning behavior now occurs in response to my need for oxygen related to holding my breath. The behavior of holding my breath happened due to worry about my test performance. In both cases, I yawned. But the reasons and what I needed were different. The communicative intent of the behavior, therefore, was different.

Learning to understand why behaviors occur is the beginning of determining the best ways to respond to and support children. Fortunately, most people demonstrate relatively consistent behavioral responses. Your child may consistently act frustrated when asked to stop playing their favorite game. Or they may always act angry if they are sleepy. These patterns emerge, and parents often intuitively begin to understand what the various behaviors are communicating. For a deeper understanding of the nuances of behavior—when the same behavior may mean different things in different situations—I recommend keeping a behavior journal. By taking note of things that happen before and after behaviors, often referred to as the antecedents and consequences, you can begin to notice the patterns in your child's behavior, as well as the different things their behavior may be trying to communicate. Table 5: Understanding Behavior and Tip Sheet 6: Keeping a Behavior Journal provide additional information to help you decode your child's typical behaviors.

Trauma and Behavior

In children impacted by complex developmental trauma and toxic stress, behavior often starts as adaptive and understandable based on the specific traumatic environment of the child. Over time, however, the adaptive behavior may become more and more maladaptive and confused. Supporting children to prevent this from happening means understanding the complex nature of the behavior and intervening to support the development of healthy response systems.

Behavior in trauma-impacted children is often a window into their internal stress responses and cognitive states. It is the complex combination of their past experiences, present emotions, and the impact of their relationships over time (Courtois, 2004; Fonseca, 2018). As these components change, so do the behaviors.

As discussed earlier, behavior serves specific functions. For a child impacted by toxic stress and trauma, behavior is all about survival, both physical and relational. Most behaviors fall into two particular categories: self-soothing and protective.

Self-soothing or self-comforting behaviors are those behaviors that help to calm or relax oneself. This often includes behaviors that activate dopamine, providing a "happy hit" whenever the behavior occurs. It

Table 5

Understanding Behavior

Behavior	What You Think It Means	What It Really Means
Yelling	• "I'm angry." • "I can't control my emotions." • "I hate it here." • "I hate you." • "I have no respect for you."	• "I'm scared." • "I don't have other ways to express my emotions." • "I'm afraid here." • "I don't feel safe." • "I am frustrated and can't communicate right now."
Frustration	• "You don't follow the rules." • "You're mad at me." • "You are choosing to be this way." • "You need me to push you more."	• "I'm scared." • "I don't have other ways to express my emotions." • "I am frustrated and can't communicate right now."
Aggressive	• "You are a mean person." • "You have poor emotional control." • "You just want to be in charge." • "You like to fight."	• "I'm scared." • "I feel deeply, but the only emotion I know how to show is anger and aggression." • "It's not safe for me to express fear or sadness, so I am aggressive when I feel everything." • "I hate fighting, but it is the only way I can be safe."
Noncompliance	• "You don't care." • "You are trying to be in control—and that's not okay." • "You don't know the rules." • "You get away with everything." • "You're spoiled."	• "I don't trust you." • "I don't feel safe." • "I'm lonely and afraid." • "I don't understand what you want." • "I don't know how to tell you what I need."

> ## Tip Sheet 6
>
> *Keeping a Behavior Journal*
>
> ---
>
> Try the following tips to keep a behavior journal and begin to decipher the meaning behind your child's behaviors.
>
> - Write the behavior that occurred, including what happened before and after the behavior.
> - Write down any ideas you have as to the communicative intent or function of the behavior.
> - Be sure to track your responses to the behavior and the impact that had on the behavior.
> - Keep a daily log initially. As you begin to decipher the behavior, you can reduce the frequency of use.
> - Use the log anytime you need to determine what the child is trying to communicate through the behavior.
>
> *Note.* Adapted from *Emotional Intensity in Gifted Students: Helping Kids Cope With Explosive Feelings* (2nd ed., p. 114), by C. Fonseca, 2016, Prufrock Press. Copyright 2016 by Prufrock Press. Adapted with permission.

may also include more dissociative behaviors. Some of the more typical behaviors that serve a self-soothing role for the trauma-impacted child include:

- sleeping,
- tech use (smartphones, video gaming),
- listening to music,
- rocking back and forth,
- substance use (marijuana and alcohol), and
- sexual behaviors.

Self-protection behaviors are behavior that helps to protect against additional threats. With toxic levels of stress, this often means protecting against anything that can result in a change or increased vulnerability. Some of the more typical behaviors used to self-protect include:

- avoidance of intimacy of any form,
- avoidance of academic risks,
- avoidance of change,
- using old patterns of behavior (the behaviors used during traumatic events), and
- isolation.

Trauma-based behavior is often a response to poor memory processing and weak emotional processes. As trauma-impacted children lose temporal orientation and begin to respond to triggers as though they are reliving the traumatic experiences, behaviors are influenced by their sensory input, environmental demands, stress loads, internal messages, and self-talk. Consider the following scenario and escalation:

A trauma-impacted high school student is sitting in a classroom at the end of the day. A problem stressed the child at lunch and left him unable to eat lunch. He is now hungry, tired, and frustrated. The teacher, unaware of the child's internal state, asks the class to turn to a specific page in a book. The child's attention isn't on the teacher, and he misses the instruction. The teacher comes over and prompts the child again, using a loud voice. This triggers the child, bringing forward a sensory memory fragment of his abusive father, who uses a similar tone of voice just before he hits the child. Immediately, the child is back in the traumatic experience of being hit. The child responds to the teacher by standing up and confronting the teacher. The teacher responds with another, more direct command to sit down or be sent to the office. The child feels even more threatened and responds by tipping his desk over and leaving class.

In this scenario, the child isn't responding to the teacher in a way consistent with the request. He is overresponding, perceiving the exchange as a threat to his survival. The teacher, then, overresponds to the child as well, seeing the initial reaction as a threat to them and their authority in the classroom. The situation escalates. If the teacher had

Table 6
Decoding Behavior

Child Behavior	Adult Feeling	Adult Response	Student Response	Student Thoughts
• Is disruptive • Makes jokes and acts out • Displays or lack of impulse control	• Irritation • Annoyance • Anger	• Remind • Coax • Reprimand • Do to the child	• Initially stops but restarts as soon as attention wanes	• "The only way I know I matter is if I am getting attention."
• Is helpless • Is scared • Is fearful	• Worry • Guilt or shame • Enmeshment	• Remind • Make excuses for the student • Do for the child	• Acts incapable • Demands more from teacher	• "I matter only when you think I need you." • "I'm not capable—you have to help me in order for me to be safe."
• Displays defiance • Is argumentative • Is passive aggressive	• Hostility • Provocation • Anger	• Force compliance • Punish • Threaten • Do to the child	• Increases behaviors • Defiance • Ups the ante	• "I matter only if I am in control." • "I have to be in control to feel safe."

Table 6, *continued*

Child Behavior	Adult Feeling	Adult Response	Student Response	Student Thoughts
• Is abusive • Is vindictive • Is self-destructive	• Hurt • Spite • Anger	• Punish • Be the victim • Retaliate • Do to the child	• Escalates behaviors • Increases intensity of behavior	• "I will never matter so I will hurt others to normalize my feelings." • "I can't be lovable, so I will hurt others to make sure that story is accurate."
• Becomes disengaged • Is indifferent • Becomes withdrawn	• Hurt • Worry • Indifference • Discouragement	• Criticize • Give up • Make excuses • Compare • Do for the child • Neglect child	• Stops working • Becomes nonresponsive • Intensifies behavior	• "I give up—I don't matter. I will never matter, so what's the point?" • "It's too scary to care about anything, so I give up . . . on everything."
• Is easily frustrated • Is aggressive • Is noncompliant	• Challenge • Provocation • Anger	• Power • Control • Get even • Punish • Do to the child	• Escalates behaviors • Increases intensity and frequency of behavior	• "Everything scares me, but the only emotion I can safely show is aggression—so that is what I do. I escalate when I am afraid."

understood the heightened state of the student, a different initial request for compliance could have been used, potentially avoiding the rest of the behavior change to occur. Table 6 provides several behavior chains and the potential beliefs behind the behaviors. Use this chart, along with Table 5, to deepen your understanding of how trauma-based behavior may show up at home and school.

Part of understanding behavior involves understanding the hidden beliefs behind the behaviors. Often children who have experienced significant traumatic events will form various assumptions about the world and the relationships in their lives. These beliefs, commonly referred to as an invisible suitcase, shape their interactions, feelings, and behaviors throughout their lifetime (The National Child Traumatic Stress Network, 2008a). Consider this example: A child's parents divorce when she is 7. Her mother, now a single parent, goes from having a lot of time to interact with the child to being tired from an exhausting job or working several jobs. She no longer has the same amount of time to interact with her daughter. The child's father has moved out of town, and she seldom sees him at all. In this scenario, the child may develop several internal beliefs for her invisible suitcase. She may think that she doesn't matter to the significant adults in her life. Or maybe she thinks she can't rely on her parents and can only rely on herself. This can translate into highly self-reliant behaviors. Or, it may result in socially avoidant behaviors. Often, the result is both. Environmental factors, EQ development, and other stressors all influence how the inner thoughts manifest as behaviors.

....

Trauma in Unique Populations

Although trauma can impact all children and adults, the potential for harm to unique populations can be particularly acute. These populations include neurologically diverse students (i.e., students with exceptional needs like autism, giftedness, and learning disabilities), students in traditionally marginalized groups (i.e., minority populations, and foster or homeless children), and students within the LGBTQ community. Increases in harm within these groups are often due to increased incidences of exposure to traumatic events (e.g., bullying), differences in how the events impact resiliency related to brain functioning (e.g., the impact of weak theory of mind conceptualization or emotional intensity), and a lack of resources available within communities (e.g., access to health care for homeless youth).

Suicidality among children of color, children with exceptional needs, and LGBTQ youth is higher than the suicidal ideations and attempts among other children by as much as 4 times the risk (The Trevor Project, 2019). Many times this increased risk is due to increased incidents of bullying. According to the National Child Traumatic Stress Network (n.d.-a), incidents of bullying can significantly impact children's self-esteem, social interactions, and school performance. Bullying can lead to increased mental health concerns, including anxiety, depression, and suicidality. Children already impacted by complex trauma are at higher risk to both perpetrate acts of bullying and be bullied by others. The negative impact of bullying can also impact trauma-impacted youth to a higher degree, resulting in PTSD and similar trauma-related mental health concerns (Idsoe et al., 2012).

In addition to the increases in bullying for many unique populations, there are differences in how some populations internalize toxic stress. Students identified as gifted, for example, may experience more intense emotional reactions to traumatic events (Fonseca, 2016). The extreme emotional response may not lead to more negative impacts related to trauma, but it can place additional stress on the developing brains and bodies of gifted children.

Similarly, students with autism may struggle with some emotional processes or interpersonal skills. The neurobiological difference in how EQ develops and how sensory information is interpreted can extend into the neurobiological impact of trauma. Understanding the unique nature of cognitive processing, motivation, and stress responses is necessary when evaluating the effect of complex developmental trauma and toxic stress on neurodiverse populations (Fuld, 2018).

Trauma-Informed Practices:
Culturally Responsive and Trauma-Informed

Becoming trauma-informed means making a switch from the idea of "What is wrong with you?" to "What may have happened to you?" (St. Andrews, 2013). Adding a culturally sensitive lens takes into consideration the culture in which the trauma occurs and emphasizes the unique experiences people have with trauma, as well as the unique ways in which people may respond. I've previously stated that people are more than their traumatic experiences. I've also said that not all people react to traumatic events in the same way. When a school becomes both trauma-informed and culturally sensitive, the school takes this into consideration.

There are many myths about trauma. You (or your child's educators or the educators you work with) may believe that all people exposed to violence need professional services to recover, or that someone exposed to many traumatic events will be in more crisis and need more support than someone exposed to a single event. Perhaps the assumptions are around cultural stereotypes. And maybe there is an assumption that trauma is perpetrated by individuals only, and not groups and institutions.

In order to be as culturally sensitive as possible when responding to trauma, you must recognize when your beliefs are anchored in myths and not facts. The truth is that people are generally very resilient and will ask for help when they need it. Furthermore, the amount of exposure to violence or other traumatic events in and of itself does not determine impact. The effect of trauma and toxic stress is related to specific neurobiological functions, social contexts, and access to resources. Each person's story is unique, and people are more than their stories of trauma. Furthermore, harm can be perpetrated not only by individuals, but also by groups and institutions (Brown, 2008).

Understanding and acknowledging these facts will help you better support children impacted by trauma.

Healing the Heart

In Chapter 6, you explored behavior as a form of communication, looking at the connection between thoughts, feelings, and actions. The chapter also discussed the impact of toxic stress on emotional development and behavior. Specific focus on trauma within unique populations was explored.

You've reviewed many of the ways complex developmental trauma and toxic stress impacts the brains and bodies of children. In the next section of *Healing the Heart*, you will examine the ways you can influence and change the outcomes for children exposed to traumatic experiences.

Heart-Centered Ideas

- Behavior is our primary communication tool.
- Behavior is the outcome of thoughts and feelings.
- Toxic stress impacts how thoughts are interpreted, affecting both emotions and behaviors.
- Trauma can significantly impact particular groups, including the LGBTQ communities, children with exceptional needs, and traditionally marginalized youth.

Healing Actions

- Maintain a behavior journal to begin to decode your child's behavior communication.
- Determine what impact, if any, trauma has had on your child's thoughts, feelings, or actions. Use Worksheet 4: My Journey Through Trauma (pp. 57–61) to jot down your ideas.

Chapter 7
Through My Eyes

Conversations With a Trauma-Impacted Teen—*Jorge's Story*

$\heartsuit$

In the later part of my career as a school psychologist, I had the honor of working at an alternative educational setting. The school housed the continuation high school, as well as the virtual and independent schools for the district. In that role, I encountered many students who had experienced trauma from one source or another. Some experienced bullying due to differences in gender or sexual identification, neurodiversity, and race or ethnicity. Some experienced adverse childhood events within the home setting. And others survived community violence or similar difficult acts. The stories these children shared have forever changed me. Together, they have taught me about the worst and best of humanity.

The following story is a combination of some of the stories shared with me in my tenure. The names have all been changed, as well as some of the identifying details. But the point of the story—the impact of trauma and the power of resiliency—remains the same. In this story, Jorge, a transgender teen whose pronoun identification is they/them, shares their story of horrific abuse, a drug overdose, and a new life. The story is raw and may trigger trauma stories of your own. I've done my best to avoid anything too graphic, while still portraying the truth of the story.

♡ ♡ ♡

My life is nothing I expected, filled with a hope and optimism I didn't think was possible even a year ago, when I was hooked on heroine and lived as a sex slave. My parents sold me into slavery when I was 13. It happened right after I told them that I wasn't really a girl, even if that was how I was born. I tried to explain that my sexual orientation and gender was far more complex than "she" or "he." They thought I was crazy, especially my dad. My version of gender didn't fit with his conservative and narrow perspective. He raped me to prove that I really was female. When that didn't magically fix my gender, he and my mom sold me to a sex slavery ring. I never understood why or how this could happen. All I knew is I was beaten unconscious and woke up one day in another place, south of the southern border of the United States. I was pumped full of drugs and repeatedly raped.

I didn't mind the drugs. They kept me numb. I didn't want to feel, didn't want to confront everything that was now true in my life. I wanted to die, end the horror that defined my existence. One day, about 3 years after I was sold, I got my chance.

I don't remember much other than the bumpy ride in the back of a large truck, and the putrid smell of too many people crammed in too small of a space. There were at least 10 of us in the truck, high and dressed for a special event—that's what they called the sex parties. When the truck stopped, we were in San Diego. I recognized the downtown skyline in the distance. Shuffled into a warehouse, we were given more drugs before being handed to whomever paid for us that night. I didn't want to do this anymore, would have given anything to end the pain I felt night after night. So I begged my "John" for more drugs. And more. He gave me anything I wanted. My world swirled and tilted until it finally went black.

I hoped I was dead. I think part of me thought I was dead. At least, until I woke up bound to a bed at my wrists and ankles. The room was too bright to be another sex den. I blinked and looked around, making out machines and people in scrubs and white coats. A hospital. I was at a hospital.

Over the next several weeks, I was given medical and psychological tests. A nurse told me that I was found in an alley in San Diego after overdosing. The authorities figured out what my parents had done, and a social worker had moved me into a lockdown facility in a neighboring state. My physical injuries, I was told, would likely heal, though they were concerned about my brain. My psychological injuries, however, could never heal fully.

I had nightmares nearly every night, reliving bits and pieces of the past several years. My days were filled with one-on-one therapy and group counseling. Counselors asked me about my life, my parents, the drugs. I didn't want to tell them everything. I didn't want to think about everything.

After 6 months, I was told that I had to leave and go home.

"Where's home?" I asked. My parents were in jail. I had no other relatives.

"California."

I was relocated into a group home and enrolled in school. How could they expect that my life could just move forward? How was I supposed to be like the other kids?

The next 3 months changed my life in the best possible way. The home I lived in was the closest thing to normal I had experienced. Part of me hated it. Most of me loved it. I had a counselor and a "coach" that helped me with school and life. I went to school for one hour each week, receiving specific work to work on at home in between my appointments at the school.

I had two teachers that helped me at the school. They were not like any teachers I remembered before—they didn't get mad when I didn't understand the work. Nor did they judge me when I asked too many questions. When I asked them to use the pronoun "they" when they referred to me, they didn't flinch at all. They seemed to accept me, something I had never experienced in any way.

My "coach" helped me complete things in between my school appointments. He had a way of explaining the work to me. With his help, I was able to complete the rest of the school year and start my last year of school. Every day got better and better with school. Every week I felt more confident and able to complete my assignments. Childhood dreams of having a good job and living in a nice apartment crept back into my thoughts. Maybe it was possible that I could have something like a "normal" life after all.

In addition to the help at school and in my group home, I also found help with my social worker. She connected me with different counselors. She helped me understand the nightmares that still continued and everything that happened over the years. I also had a CASA worker (a Court Appointed Special Advocates volunteer) that was like a parent to me. My CASA worker connected me to different community people who could train me for a job and help me when I turned 18.

It's been 2 years since I came back to California. I feel better than I've ever felt. For the first time, I believe that I can have the life I dreamed of as a child—I can get a job (maybe in computers— turns out I am really good at programming), get an apartment, and find a life after everything that has happened to me. I still have bad dreams. I still worry that the drugs damaged my brain permanently, despite the tests that say I'm fine. The things I've lived through will probably never leave me. My trauma-related PTSD still causes panic attacks. But, I've learned how to manage my emotions now. I have come to call myself a survivor. I realize that although I have had to endure things most people will never experience, I am much more than the things that have happened to me.

I am grateful for the many people in my life that have helped me to heal—the teachers, the counselors, the coaches, the psychologists, the students, and more. Each of these people have taught me how to live again. Through them, I've learned to hope, to dream.

Jorge's story is one of the most poignant I've ever experienced. Their survival happened because of all of the people who were willing to see past their trauma. They helped Jorge redefine their life. Through the positive connections developed between the adults and Jorge, new beliefs were built. Jorge began to believe that they could have a new life. Eventually, they did.

The next section of *Healing the Heart* provides many of the strategies and interventions that helped Jorge and others move from barely surviving traumatic events to thriving in spite of the experiences. You will learn how to reestablish safety and build connections that will help your child heal the negative impact of trauma on both the mind and the body.

Part III
Rebuilding Safety

This section begins the shift from information about trauma to the specific ways being trauma-informed can start to protect and support children impacted by the adverse effects of traumatic events. Over the next several chapters, you will learn specific ways to rebuild a safety net for children, develop healthy relationships with those impacted by toxic stress, and start the process of healing.

Throughout the following chapters are tips and strategies that focus on helping children move through the story of their trauma and into healing. Topics include (1) creating safe environments, (2) rebuilding trust and security, (3) navigating boundaries, and (4) recognizing and responding to trauma triggers. Specific guidance for seeking support through schools and mental health professionals is included, as well as evidence-based strategies for parents.

The section ends with an interview with several middle school students about community trauma and its impacts on their lives. Through this chapter, kernels of hope can be seen in the darkest of events as several students now rebuild their lives after events within the community threaten their families.

Chapter 8
Creating Safety

♡

Now that you have a clear understanding of the types of traumatic events children experience and the impact of those experiences on developing brains and bodies, it is time to start the process of healing. In order for children or adults to reframe their stories of trauma, reboot the stress response back into something adaptive, and regulate emotional responses, it is imperative to feel a sense of safety.

But what does it mean to be safe? This chapter examines safety and security in all of its forms and provides strategies to help you rebuild safety for the entire family community.

What Is Safety?

The beginnings of healing from traumatic events and their impact begin with safety, both physical and psychological. As easy as this may sound on the surface, it is often one of the most challenging aspects of post-trauma healing.

Physical safety is defined as the state of being safe from harm. Establishing safety means establishing environments in which there is a reasonable expectation that you will be safe from harm to your body.

Although no situation is 100% guaranteed to be safe, creating a home environment in which the children feel secure is necessary to heal from the impact of trauma. Safe environments are those in which:

- violent behavior does not occur,
- access to weapons is minimized through the use of appropriate precautions, and
- adequate availability of healthy food, clean drinking water, sleep, exercise, health care, and positive connections with trusted, caring adults is prioritized.

When there are challenges to physical safety, as in the case of poverty, abuse within the home setting, or engagement in self-harm and addiction behaviors, the barriers need to be addressed and rectified for healing to occur.

Note that even if all of the components of physical safety are in place, real safety cannot occur without psychological safety. Psychological safety refers to the state of feeling heard, seen, cared for, and connected to trusted and caring adults in one's life. When you experience psychological safety, you can interact with others without feeling like you will be rejected. At school, this often means a child can take academic risks and learn. At home, this may mean that a child feels like they have a voice and some agency.

For children and adults who have experienced traumatic events, heightened perceptions of danger and vulnerability are common. Establishing both physical and psychological safety is a necessary first step in growth after the traumatic events.

Safety Begins Inside

As I mentioned earlier, there is no way to be 100% safe in this world. You cannot control the actions of others, nor can you fully insolate yourself against adverse experiences. You are vulnerable to things that can threaten safety. Everyone is; it is part of the shared human experience. However, there are many things you can do to create security for yourself and your children. And there are many things you can teach your children to do to improve their perceptions of both physical and psychological safety.

The establishment of safety begins, according to leading trauma expert Judith Herman (2015), with the body and mind, and moves outward to the environment. For you and your children, this means working on mindset and social-emotional development. Work together to develop an emotional vocabulary. Label different feelings as you experience them. Help your children label their feelings. Create an emotion wheel that highlights nuanced and blended behaviors. Through these diagrams, your children can begin to develop the language necessary to explain and recover from intense feelings. Using such diagrams will also start to repair lateral communication in the brain, changing the way the brain functions and improving any deterioration caused by toxic stress. Worksheet 5: Wheel of Emotion can assist you in helping your child develop their own wheel of emotion. See Figure 1 for a complete example.

Building emotional literacy is key to recovery from trauma, as well as the development of resiliency resources. Tip Sheet 7: Developing Emotional Literacy provides several recommendations for ways to help children develop their emotional language skills.

In addition to developing emotional language, you need to help your children develop emotional regulation skills. As discussed previously, behavior happens at the end of the thinking-feeling-behavior chain. In a child impacted by trauma, explosive behavior is often the result of destructive thinking and the corresponding intense feelings. The thinking creates internalized threats to safety. The emotions and actions that follow are the child's attempt to reestablish some form of internal safety through any means necessary. Disrupting this pattern starts with recognizing and interrupting the destructive thinking.

Think of thoughts as a television show. Interrupting the thinking is just like changing the channel on the television. Children can often use the visualization of using a television remote control to change the TV channel as a way to imagine changing their thoughts. Using internal dialogue scripts, like "Stop that" or "I can think differently," is another technique that can work to interrupt destructive thinking patterns. Of

Worksheet 5
Wheel of Emotion

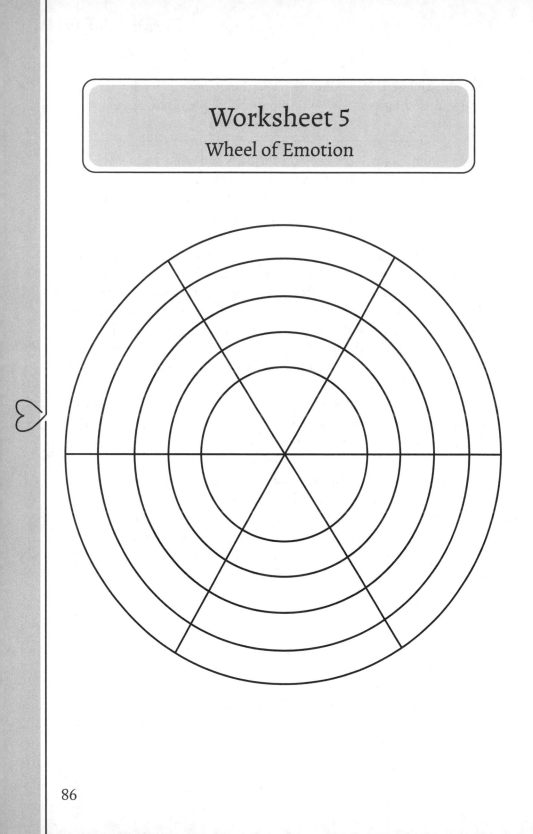

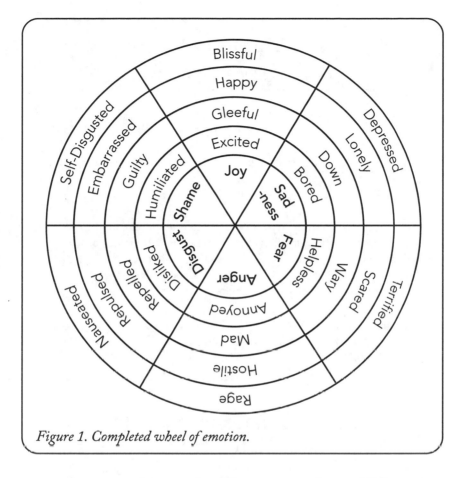

Figure 1. Completed wheel of emotion.

course, these strategies can only work once you and your children recognize the connection between thoughts, feelings, and behaviors and can identify destructive thinking patterns. Worksheet 6: Thinking About My Behavior can help you and your children begin to identify and change thinking patterns.

Identifying and changing unhelpful thinking takes a while to learn. But as you and your children develop the self-awareness skills needed, internalized emotional regulation begins to emerge. Every time you successfully shift thinking and change behavior, you begin to recreate scripts of safety in your thoughts. As internal security grows, additional post-traumatic growth begins to occur. You have started on the path of recovery and healing.

Tip Sheet 7

Developing Emotional Literacy

o Pair feelings with words.
o For each feeling, pick a word. Help the child define what that word means.
o Draw pictures and/or make cards for the emotional vocabulary if the child is young.
o Encourage using the new emotional vocabulary on a consistent basis.
o Use the emotion wheel as a way to deepen emotional literacy.
o Talk about emotions in characters from books and movies as a way to build fluency in emotional literacy (e.g., "What do you think that character is feeling?", "Why do you think she feels that way?", "How would you feel in that situation?").

Note. Adapted from *Raising the Shy Child: A Parent's Guide to Social Anxiety* (p. 40) by C. Fonseca, 2015, Prufrock Press. Copyright 2015 by Prufrock Press. Adapted with permission.

The Foundations of a Safe and Caring Home

Establishing inner safety through the development of social-emotional skills is the beginning of recovery. For the initial healing to take hold, an environment of safety is also necessary. You can do many things to create safe environments for your children. Start by ensuring physical safety, as described earlier in the chapter. Once the essential physical safety components are addressed, focus on emotional safety.

Emotional safety is created through parental relationships. Establish clear expectations for behavior, with appropriate consequences for appropriate and inappropriate behaviors. Consistently follow the established expectations and consequences. The more predictable your behavioral reactions to your children, the safer your children will feel. When

Worksheet 6
Thinking About My Behavior

Directions: Think about a difficult and unhelpful behavior you do. Ask yourself the following:

- When do I typically engage in this behavior?
- How do I feel before, during, and after the behavior?
- What thoughts do I have before, during, and after the behavior?

After thinking through a few behaviors, write your thoughts in the following table.

What Is the Behavior?	What Are Your Feelings?	What Are Your Thoughts?	Any Other Observations?

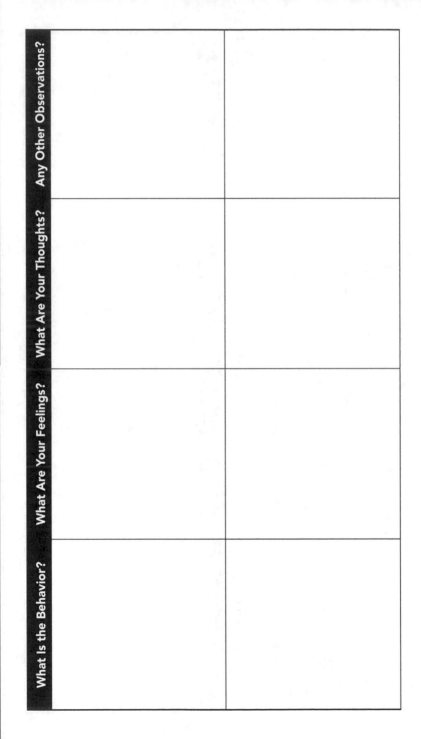

What Is the Behavior?	What Are Your Feelings?	What Are Your Thoughts?	Any Other Observations?

What Is the Behavior?	What Are Your Feelings?	What Are Your Thoughts?	Any Other Observations?

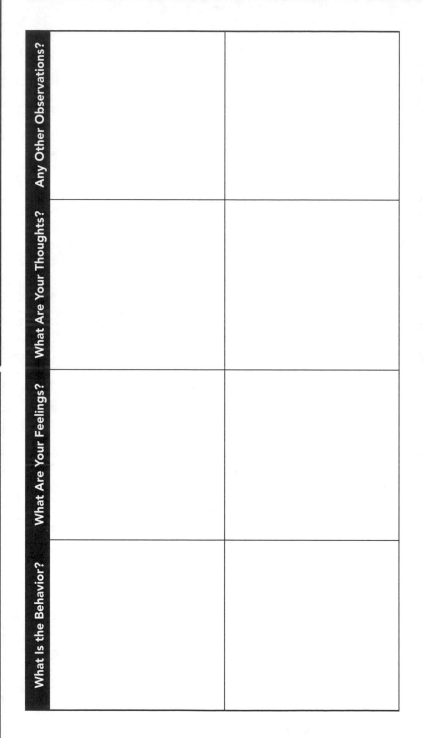

What Is the Behavior?	What Are Your Feelings?	What Are Your Thoughts?	Any Other Observations?

What Is the Behavior?	What Are Your Feelings?	What Are Your Thoughts?	Any Other Observations?

you respond in predictable ways, your children learn to trust their social environments. This is crucial for recovery. Your trauma-impacted children may struggle with trust as they are less able to construct predictability from their world. If you respond in highly consistent ways to their behavior, they can repair the damage that may have been caused to memory and emotional processing. They begin to learn what actions lead to what consequences. They can start to reconstruct meaning from their social environments. As this occurs, trust begins to form. Through trust comes safety.

If you are a trauma-impacted adult, you may have difficulty engaging in predictable patterns of behavior. You may struggle with destructive thought patterns just as your children do. You may distrust your social environment and lack emotional safety, as well. If this is true for you, start by establishing internal safety. Develop your self- and social awareness skills, and begin to pay attention to your tone of voice and emotional states when interacting with your children. If you notice that you struggle to maintain emotional control, admit that to your children. Let them know you are practicing the skill, but you may struggle at times, just like they do. Work together to identify times when the family is good at communicating and meeting expectations, and times when family members struggle. Enlist the help of a therapist if you are unable to manage your emotional responses.

Learning how to establish both internal and external psychological safety is possible. It may feel awkward, and it may take time. But your children's post-traumatic growth is dependent on helping them establish their safety. Your establishment of inner and outer safety is a needed first step. Tip Sheet 8: Psychological Safety at Home highlights several ways you can create psychological safety for your children.

....

Social-Emotional Learning and Trauma

One of the most exciting bodies of research in positive psychology is the research regarding social-emotional learning (SEL) and its impact on overall functioning. Based on several research studies, as children develop social and emotional processes, improvements are

Tip Sheet 8

Psychological Safety at Home

Directions: Try the following tips to create an emotionally safe environment at home.

○ Listen first. Listen often.
○ Define expectations and consequences for good and not-so-good behavior.
○ Allow space for emotional reactions.
○ Avoid making assumptions about your child's thoughts or feelings.
○ Focus on developing strong connections with your child.
○ Be willing to be vulnerable.
○ Develop healthy boundaries.
○ Model good emotional regulation skills.

seen in lateral and vertical communication centers of the brain. With these improvements, children improve in emotional literacy, emotional regulation, social awareness, and relationship skills (Durlak et al., 2015; Mahoney et al., 2018).

I was excited when I read the research. The impact of complex developmental trauma and toxic stress on children is significant. The damages caused by fractured communication and diminished integration laterally and vertically in the brain can adversely impact a child for life. But the research into social-emotional learning skills suggests that this condition is not permanent. Children can learn about social-emotional and cognitive processing skills. Children can rebuild the integration of the brain and experience higher levels of SEL skill development and improved resilience. Tip Sheet 9: Building SEL Skills at Home provides several ways you and other caregivers can improve the outcomes for children impacted by trauma through SEL skill development.

Tip Sheet 9
Building SEL Skills at Home

- Work on building an emotional vocabulary.
- Model and teach prosocial skills.
- Practice perspective-taking skills. Use literature and other media to explore other points of view.
- Develop a menu of coping strategies to handle trauma triggers.
- Teach creative problem-solving skills and conflict resolution skills.
- Develop and practice oral communication skills.
- Celebrate successes often.

Note. Adapted from Fonseca, 2015.

Trauma-Informed Practices:
The Trauma-Sensitive Classroom

A stressed-out brain doesn't learn. When a child is impacted by complex developmental trauma and toxic stress, the capacity to learn and retain information is significantly impaired. The mind is focused on survival. Hypersensitive threat awareness sees danger around every corner, as the trauma-impacted child continually scans the environment for potential harm. Some children dissociate from the situation altogether, unable to engage in the social or learning aspects of school. Developing safe places at school—classrooms that promote a caring and trusting environment—is vital to help students who have experienced traumatic events move past what happened to them and toward healing.

Researchers have identified four critical components to a trauma-sensitive classroom: (1) healthy, caring relationships between adults and children, (2) clearly defined expectations for behavior, (3) predictability from adults and within the environment, and (4) opportunities for student choice and voice. These components help establish safety for students, the foundation of recovery (Fonseca, 2019; St. Andrews, 2013).

Developing caring relationships with students is vital for all students. With those impacted by traumatic events, a healthy, caring relationship does more than assist in creating a safe, trusting environment in which students can learn and take academic risks. Positive relationships help to rebuild resiliency. Students can learn to trust. Positive relationships between adults and students happen when the adults understand the potential impact of trauma on the students and see that the students have more than what happened to them. A focus is placed on learning about students' lives beyond their academic performance. Educators are authentic with students and express caring through positive interactions. Time is spent listening to students with a goal of deep understanding. Opportunities for student participation, including voice and choice about their learning, are invited and welcomed. As the opportunities increase and the relationship between the educator and students grow, students learn to trust their learning environment.

Educators must understand that students impacted by trauma may struggle to form appropriate relationships. They may lack any internal definition of what an appropriate relationship looks and feels like. They may also engage in sabotaging behavior when they experience a healthy relationship, pushing the teacher away. This often happens due to discomfort and a lack of trust on the part of a student. They may feel vulnerable as they begin to trust the adult. That vulnerability may communicate threat and ignite the cycle of trauma so familiar to them.

Note that is it common for students impacted by trauma to be triggered by everyday experiences at school. A specific sensory event (e.g., a scent, sound, or particular phrase) can easily trigger traumatic memories and feelings. Students will rarely be able to explain what is happening in these moments, and the behavior they often exhibit can be confusing. Refer to the Table 6 (p. 70) to help decipher the students' behavioral response. Tip Sheet 18: Deescalating Students (p. 153) may give you additional strategies to help students move past their triggers and regulate their behavior.

As more and more students come to school impacted by trauma and toxic levels of stress, creating a trauma-sensitive learning environment is necessary to best serve our students. Tip Sheet 10: Creating a Trauma-Sensitive Classroom provides more ways to support students.

Tip Sheet 10

Creating a Trauma-Sensitive Classroom

A trauma-sensitive classroom includes the following components.

○ Teacher-student relationships should be:
- caring,
- trusting,
- respectful, and
- responsive.

○ A safe and efficacious environment includes:
- opportunities for academic and personal mastery of skills,
- modeling of healthy coping and problem-solving strategies,
- offering a high degree of positive performance feedback, and
- celebrations of success throughout the classroom.

○ Healthy peer connections should be promoted through:
- engaging learning activities,
- opportunities to learn about each other,
- classroom community-building activities,
- explicit teaching of conflict resolution and social problem-solving skills, and
- expectations for inclusionary behavior.

In addition to building the relationship between students and adults, helping students feel safe in the classroom is essential. This occurs when expectations are clearly and regularly defined. This helps students understand what to expect within the class and how they are expected to act. Predictable responses from teachers solidify the safety within the room. Further, they help to rebuild the emotional processes and memory scripts in students' stress-impacted brains.

Through these components, students with complex developmental trauma begin to rebuild trust in their social environments. They begin to understand cause-effect relationships and begin to navigate their world successfully. Each time this happens, students' confidence in their inner thoughts improves. Over time, the healthy relationships and safe, predictable environments at school can repair the damage caused by the initial traumatic events. The vicious cycles described in Part II are disrupted, and healing occurs.

Healing the Heart

In Part III, the focus has shifted from understanding trauma to knowing what to do to move past the traumas. Chapter 8 focused on the idea of safety—physical, emotional, and psychological. Throughout the chapter, you learned ways to instill a feeling of safety and security for your children, without accidentally creating dependency and overreliance.

Heart-Centered Ideas

- Humans need to feel safe physically, emotionally, and psychologically in order to thrive.
- Safety can be found even in unsafe situations.
- Safety comes through the development of resilience, self-reliance, and emotional intelligence.
- Learning to embrace all emotions and find the strength-message in each can help you support your children in feeling safe and secure.
- Learning occurs when there is a balance between security and informed risk.

Healing Actions

- Review the tips and strategies throughout the chapter and choose two you will try with your children.
- Take a moment to reflect on the chapter and complete the safety inventory, located on Worksheet 4: My Journey Through Trauma (pp. 57–61).

Chapter 9
Relationships Matter

$\heartsuit$

According to Harvard University's Center on the Developing Child (n.d.), one of the most important factors in the development of resilience in children is the presence of at least one positive and committed relationship with a significant adult in the child's life. Humans are hardwired to benefit from connections and a sense of belonging. Not only does a person's survival rate increase, but also they flourish. Social-emotional development improves through relationships, and resilience toward adversity is enhanced.

In this chapter, you will explore how positive relationships are impacted by trauma and how they are reformed and maintained long after the traumatic events have passed.

Healthy Relationships Defined

The National Scientific Council on the Developing Child (2004) highlighted the importance of supportive relationships to the healthy development of children's brain structures. Children's brains develop within a social context of relationships and the ability to form healthy bonds with other people. Through healthy relationships between children and adults, especially primary caregivers, children learn to trust their internal and external worlds. Safety is established, emotional processes are developed, and the brain integrates to a high degree. The relationship between children and a caring adult can lead to the best possible outcomes in learning, SEL skill development, and overall physical, mental, and emotional health.

Healthy relationships in early childhood refer to adult-child relationships that are nurturing, reliable, and stimulating (National Scientific Council on the Developing Child, 2004). Within this type of relationship, caregivers and other adults are predictable and consistent in their responses to children. They interact with children, signing, talking, and engaging directly. Passive activities do not establish the same kind of bond as interactive activities. Watching a movie together, for example, doesn't engage and nurture the relationship the way the conversations to and from the movie might.

In children impacted by ACEs, it is possible that positive relationships were not available. A child may not have experienced healthy attachment. The lack of social engagement may have significantly delayed some aspects of brain development. As the child begins to heal and recover from the experiences, refocusing on relationships and attachment is essential. Parents or other caregivers may need some help to learn how to engage with their children and reform relationships appropriately. Fortunately, research indicates that it is possible to repair household relationships (Arneson, 2015).

It will likely take work, but developing healthy relationships between you and your children is possible. Focus on interacting with your child. Demonstrate unconditional love, acceptance, and respect. Learn to respond in predictable and consistent ways to your child's behaviors. Develop structure and consistency in the home. Provide for the safety of your child, both physically and psychologically. All of these things can create a healthy relationship and begin both of you on the path of post-traumatic growth.

The Gift of Boundaries

A critical aspect of healthy relationships is the development of boundaries. Boundaries define the limits of things. In relationships between adults and children, boundaries help to teach children where they begin and end and where the adult starts and ends. Healthy boundaries communicate to children that there are limits to acceptable behavior, lines that should not be crossed. Boundaries teach social awareness to children, helping them learn that other people exist and have needs, wants, and ideas separate from those of the children. Boundaries help to develop "theory of mind," a necessary component to the healthy development of empathy.

Consider this scenario:

A child forgets to study for a test. In the morning, she remembers the test and panics. She begs you, her parent, to let her miss the test. You feel bad for her, and you don't want an argument, so you allow her to miss school and the test. All day you feel bad, ashamed for caving in to her. When you get home, you expect to find her remorseful. Instead, she has spent the day on her phone and not studying. You explode with anger.

What happened in this scenario? Was this an issue of boundaries? Something else? You allowed the child to avoid a consequence to both give her a break and avoid conflict. All day you felt her feelings for her, becoming distressed. When you discovered that she didn't feel the shame or guilt you felt, you got mad—she failed to live up to your expectations.

All of this could have been avoided by maintaining expectations and emotional boundaries. Allow the child to experience the consequences of her actions, maintain emotional boundaries by not owning her feelings for her, and help her understand the choices she made and the implications of those choices.

Establishing and maintaining boundaries occurs with the following steps (Fonseca, 2019):

- setting clear expectations for behavior;

- using consistent consequences for behavioral missteps;
- reacting with consistent adult emotional responses;
- supporting, but not rescuing, your children;
- redefining failures as opportunities for growth; and
- accepting that negative emotions are not inherently bad.

Each step helps you and your child establish healthy limits. With these limits in place, it is easier to form and maintain beneficial relationships.

If you are also recovering from trauma, some of the steps may be difficult for you. You may struggle to understand where your emotions start and stop, and where your child's feelings start and stop. You may be entangled in your child's emotional happiness. If this is true, you may want to enlist the help of mental health professionals to help you move into a healthier perspective and establish boundaries. Without clear limits, it is much easier to become overwhelmed by your child's behavior, react emotionally instead of intentionally, and easily trigger your trauma story.

Strategies That Help Heal From Trauma

There are several strategies and practices that can help children and adults recover and heal from trauma and the impact of toxic stress. These practices help to build resiliency skills and improve the brain's lateral and vertical integration.

One of the most promising practices is mindfulness. Often defined as present moment awareness, mindfulness practices help children and adults learn to attend to present thoughts, motivations, and behaviors. Mindfulness is the foundation for many therapeutic treatments for trauma, including cognitive behavioral therapy (CBT), acceptance-commitment therapy (ACT), integrative trauma treatments, and others. Through the practice of mindfulness, adults and children can learn to identify and respond to trauma triggers in healthy ways, identify errors in trauma memories, regulate emotional reactions, and neutralize the damaging impact of toxic stress (Raja, 2012; St. Andrews, 2013).

Mindfulness involves noticing the input from your five senses; watching your thoughts and feelings without judgment or action; labeling thoughts, attitudes, and behaviors separate from one another; and focusing on one thing at a time. Tip Sheet 11: Mindfulness Practice lists several activities you can use to build your mindfulness skills.

In addition to mindfulness practices, learning strategies to identify and correct cognitive errors is also essential to post-trauma recovery. Cognitive errors refer to mistaken assumptions you might make as a result of the "story" going on in your head. With trauma, this story is often written by the thoughts in your invisible suitcase. Learning to recognize the mistake in thinking means unpacking the information in your invisible suitcase and discerning helpful from nonhelpful thinking, as well as accurate from inaccurate thinking. Once corrections are made, the suitcase can be repacked with accurate and useful thoughts. Worksheet 7: Correcting Thought Patterns provides some strategies for correcting cognition errors.

No conversation about post-trauma recovery is complete without teaching specific stress reduction strategies. This is especially important in the beginning phases of recovery, while emotions are often raw and intense. Stress reduction strategies, or coping strategies, involve specific productive actions a person can use when triggered to reduce the anxiety caused by the triggering incident. Without a particular set of strategies for coping with trauma triggering events, an impacted person will often engage in destructive behaviors that help them dissociate from the painful feelings and anxiety. This will often lead to less mindfulness, more cognitive errors, and reduced resilience. By utilizing more effective coping strategies, a person can grow resilience while reducing anxiety and lessening the difficult emotions. Breathing techniques, body relaxation strategies, and journaling are all proven strategies for reducing the stress in healthy, nondestructive ways. Tip Sheet 22: Coping With Stress (p. 166) provides several calming strategies than can help reduce the negative impact of triggering events.

Mental health professionals have several promising treatments available to treat children impacted by complex developmental trauma and toxic stress. Table 7 lists some of the most common therapeutic approaches and descriptions of the essential components. This list is

---

Tip Sheet 11

Mindfulness Practice

---

o **Mindful Breathing:** Close your eyes and take a deep, slow breath through your nose. Hold briefly and exhale through your mouth. Continue for several minutes.

o **Mindful Walking:** Take a morning walk or hike. Focus fully on the act of walking. How does your body feel as it moves through the space? What does the air smell like? How does the wind or sun feel?

o **Mindful Moments:** Take a moment and find a place where you can be quiet for a few minutes. Close your eyes and inhale a few deep breaths. Focus on your body. Where are you feeling tension? Concentrate your focus on those areas, imagining your body releasing the tightness in your muscles and fully relaxing. Do this with each area of tension until you feel fully relaxed. Continue for a minute or so until your mind is clear, and your body is relaxed.

Note. Adapted from *The Caring Child: Raising Empathetic and Emotionally Intelligent Children* (pp. 68–69), by C. Fonseca, 2019, Prufrock Press. Copyright 2019 by Prufrock Press. Adapted with permission.

not exhaustive. It merely provides you with general information as to available treatments commonly utilized with mental health professionals. Consult with your mental health provider when considering the most appropriate approach for your specific situation. For complete, up-to-date information about current treatments, refer to the resources provided on the National Child Traumatic Stress Network website (http://www.nctsn.org).

Worksheet 7
Correcting Thought Patterns

Directions: Think about your inaccurate or unhelpful thoughts and complete the following:

Inaccurate or Unhelpful Thought	Why It Is Inaccurate or Unhelpful	Empowering or Helpful Thought
Example: My father hits me because I am bad.	*I am just a child. Regardless of what I've done, hitting isn't okay. I don't deserve to be hit.*	*My father hits when he's angry. He doesn't manage his anger effectively.*

Inaccurate or Unhelpful Thought	Why It Is Inaccurate or Unhelpful	Empowering or Helpful Thought

Note. Adapted from *Letting Go: A Girl's Guide to Breaking Free of Stress and Anxiety* (p. 82), by C. Fonseca, 2017, Prufrock Press. Copyright 2017 by Prufrock Press. Adapted with permission.

Table 7

Best Practices in Trauma Treatment

Treatment Name	Objectives
Trauma-Focused Cognitive Behavioral Therapy (TF-CBT)	• Reduce levels of anxiety, depression, and/or dissociation symptoms
Attachment, Self-Regulation, and Competency (ARC)	• Reduce symptoms of anxiety, depression, and dissociation • Increase adaptive and social skills • Reduce distress with caregivers • Reframe behaviors as less dysfunctional
Integrated Treatment of Complex Trauma	• Decrease symptoms of depression, anxiety, anger, PTSD, and internal and external symptoms • Increase self-regulation, self-esteem, and self-efficacy
Dialectical Behavioral Therapy (DBT)	• Use mindfulness to reduce anxiety and depression, increase coping and regulation skills, and build resilience
Acceptance and Commitment Therapy (ACT)	• Combine mindfulness with CBT; build acceptance of personal experiences, reframe thinking, develop self-awareness and regulation, identify goals and values, and commit to recovery process
Somatic Experiencing	• Discharge neurological memory of the traumatic experience stored within the body • Rebuild EQ and resilience
Eye Movement Desensitization and Reprocessing (EMDR)	• Use repetitive eye movements to overwrite trauma memories with more adaptive beliefs, emotions, and somatic responses • Reduce toxic stress and anxiety

Note. Adapted from the National Child Traumatic Stress Network, n.d.-b.

Healing the Heart

In addition to feeling safe and secure, children impacted by trauma need support in developing positive relationships. Chapter 9 focused on defining relationships and understanding the role of boundaries. Additional information was given about the foundation skills needed to begin post-trauma healing.

Trauma-Informed Practices:
Resilience—A Buffer to Trauma

ACEs research indicates that developing resilience in children can buffer the harmful effects of adverse childhood experiences and help children lead healthy and productive lives. In the school setting, developing resilience is rooted in the same components as trauma-sensitive classrooms, including safety, positive relationships, and student agency. Additionally, teachers can engage in several specific behaviors that will help students develop resiliency skills. These include:

- modeling appropriate emotional regulation,
- modeling problem-solving skills,
- teaching self-motivation and self-reliance skills,
- checking in with students regularly,
- being culturally sensitive and responsive, and
- explicitly teaching and modeling SEL skills.

Each of the listed behaviors helps students practice necessary social-emotional learning skills, as well as deepen their integration of these skills in the brain. As the skills integrate, resiliency is enhanced.

Furthermore, teacher behaviors help students develop trust and a sense of belonging within the school climate. Students begin to internalize control over their thoughts, feelings, and actions. The damaging cycle of toxic stress ends, and mental wellness grows.

Heart-Centered Ideas

- All humans need positive, healthy relationships in order to flourish.
- Relationship skills are often compromised as a result of trauma.
- Developing healthy relationships requires setting and observing boundaries, navigating conflict, and developing perspective taking.

Healing Actions

- Review the tips and strategies in the chapter. Commit to using one or two with your children.
- Write you action plan for using the strategy or tip in the appropriate chapter section of Worksheet 4: My Journey Through Trauma (pp. 57–61).

Chapter 10
Seeing Past the Trauma

♡

___

Healing the heart happens only when you and your children can see beyond the story of your trauma. As I've mentioned many times throughout the book, our internal stories determine our feelings and behaviors. Changing the story is key to changing how you feel about the traumatic events and how those events continue to impact your life. This is true for adults and children. Chapter 10 focuses on ways to move beyond the circumstances and rewrite the story of these events in your hearts and minds. This provides the foundation necessary to move from surviving to the final section of the book—thriving.

Post-traumatic Growth

As children and adults begin to recover and heal from the impact of trauma exposure and toxic stress, they begin to experience post-traumatic growth. The trauma survivor begins to find meaning in the trauma and learn about themselves and their strengths. They begin to rewrite the impact of the trauma and apply newly acquired social-emotional skills to change previous ways of responding to the trauma. This doesn't mean that children and adults no longer experience intense emotions related to the trauma—they often do. Post-traumatic growth simply means that they can recognize the feelings, reframe responses, and move forward (St. Andrews, 2013).

Post-traumatic growth often includes increases in emotional processes (i.e., emotional literacy and regulation), interpersonal processes (i.e., relationship skills and prosocial behavior), cognitive regulation (i.e., attention and behavior inhibition), and mindset. This is due to improvements in both lateral and vertical communication and integration in the brain. The various strategies discussed throughout the book and in the next section help foster the growth as well. Factors like a safe environment, positive relationships, boundaries, and skill development all lead to significant, positive shifts for the trauma-impacted person.

As children initially begin to demonstrate post-traumatic growth, recognize the changes and separate the growth from the trauma itself. The trauma survivor must understand that although the experience created the opportunities to grow, the destructive event isn't the cause of the growth.

There are many ways parents can help children experience post-traumatic growth. Helping to build social-emotional learning skills, encouraging and practicing coping strategies, and nurturing a growth mindset all help support growth. Setting emotional boundaries and prosocial norms is essential as well. Prosocial norms are specific rules around self-destructive behaviors. It is crucial to emphasize appropriate coping strategies and positive, healthy relationships (Calhoun & Tedeschi, 2014).

Gratitude and Forgiveness

Another great way to promote post-traumatic growth is through the development of gratitude and forgiveness. Gratitude and forgiveness have been cited by researchers as skills that not only support an optimistic mindset but also reduce feelings of anxiety and the negative impact of stress (Fonseca, 2017). They increase the brain's serotonin and dopamine levels, promote positive social and emotional processes, and enhance resiliency.

Developing gratitude can begin with the simple act of finding something to be grateful for every day. In trauma-impacted children, I recommend having them finding something to be thankful for at home, at school, and within themselves. Some days this will be difficult. Very difficult. Teach children that they can find something small.

I remember one child I worked with started off being grateful for things like getting to school or remembering her homework. As time progressed, her list began to include things like completing her homework, making a new friend, and practicing her mindfulness skills. Eventually, the list started to include more personal things, like recognizing a trauma trigger and managing her emotions. With each gratitude practice, the student began to feel comfortable looking for positive things and feeling gratitude. Optimism developed, as well as hope for the future.

The development of forgiveness skills may also be difficult for some children. Begin by helping children to understand what forgiveness is and is not. Explain that forgiveness is not about ignoring feelings like anger. It is about choosing to release the hold of anger, to no longer allow the actions of another person to dictate how they feel. Forgiveness and reconciliation are not the same. Harm is real, and when it has been created, it may take time and action to repair the damage. Forgiveness is not for the person who committed the harm—forgiveness is for the person harmed, a chance to decide to release painful emotions.

After teaching children about forgiveness, practice identifying acts of forgiveness. You can use books and movies for this step. Discuss how the characters forgave and the things they did. Once children can identify what forgiveness is and have examples of how to forgive, they are ready to practice the skill. Start with something small. Invite the child to think about something they are still upset about and ready to release. Ask them to write down the situation. The child can read their story aloud to you. Talk about what harm was created by the event and what is needed to reconcile that harm. No matter what harm was created and whether or not things have yet been repaired, invite the child to forgive the other person. If they are ready, ask them to say, "I forgive _____ for _____. I choose to release my anger (or other feelings) and move forward." Tip Sheet 12: Practicing Forgiveness outlines each step in the process. As your child gets better at practicing forgiveness, they will learn that although they can't control what happens to them, they can choose how to manage their thoughts and feelings about the events.

. . . .

The Power of Superhero Stories

One of the most promising approaches to treat trauma and toxic stress in children and adolescents is Superhero Therapy. This technique, developed by Janine Scarlet (2019), combines pop culture and fandoms with conventional therapeutic approaches like CBT and ACT. Using the characters from various fandoms, children explore their origin stories (the traumatic events), monsters (negative thoughts, feelings, and behaviors), core values, and resources (superpowers). Children connect the stories of their favorite superheroes to their lives. They find social connections, build skills, and create anchors to help reframe experiences.

The research in the use of fandoms to support mental health is exciting. Researchers have found reductions in social isolation, improved compassion and empathy development, and growth in prosocial behaviors (Scarlet, 2019). Using superhero poses (i.e., Superman or Wonder Woman pose) has been found to boost self-confidence and optimism and combat social anxiety (Peña & Chen, 2017).

The next time your child dives into their favorite fandom, talk with them about what makes them like the characters. Who do they most identify with? What values does that character demonstrate? Draw on the strengths of the characters to help your child see their own strengths. Through the power of superhero stories, your child can find their own strengths and move from their painful origin story to claim their superpower.

. . . .

Tip Sheet 12

Practicing Forgiveness

Try these steps to develop a practice of forgiveness.

1. Teach the concept of forgiveness.
2. Identify forgiveness skills in characters from stories in books or movies.
3. Have the child identify an experience that upset them and that they are ready to release.
4. Ask the child to write down the details of the event, including what happened, who did it, how it made the child feel, and what they hoped would happen.
5. Ask the child to read the story aloud.
6. Discuss the harm that the event created and what the child would need for things to be made "right."
7. Ask the child to identify any strong emotions associated with the event.
8. Ask the child if they are ready to release the strong negative emotions.
9. If the child is ready, ask the child to say "I forgive _____ for _____. I choose to release my anger (or other feelings) and move forward."

Trauma-Informed Practices: The Impact of Helping

Working with children impacted by trauma can have a significant impact on adult "helpers," including parents, educators, mental health providers, and anyone assisting communities after a crisis. The terms *vicarious trauma*, *secondary traumatic stress*, and *compassion fatigue* are often used interchangeably to refer to the negative stress response that may occur in adults who work with children impacted by trauma. Although different, each term tries to capture the risks to oneself that occur when empathizing with students who've experienced trauma.

Vicarious trauma refers to the changes in one's thinking that may occur after working with survivors of trauma (Newell & MacNeil, 2010). Such changes typically involving a difference in threat perception, concepts of safety, and even spiritual beliefs. The changes are generally detrimental and are similar to initial cognitive shifts in the primary survivors of trauma. Many of the first responders to the 9/11 terrorist attacks suffered vicarious trauma, changing their worldview regarding safety and acts of terrorism.

Secondary traumatic stress is a high level of stress that occurs after significant others, clients, or anyone with whom you have an empathetic relationship survives trauma. This type of stress often mirrors PTSD in scope and intensity (Newell & MacNeil, 2010). This type of stress is made worse if you have underdeveloped empathy skills, especially in the area of boundaries and theory of mind. This type of immature empathy frequently leads to emotional distress as you tend to take on the emotions of others—something particularly detrimental in the case of a trauma (Fonseca, 2019).

Compassion fatigue is similar to secondary traumatic stress in that helpers often present with PTSD-like symptoms, including apathy, irritability, fatigue, motivation difficulties, overwhelm, depression-like symptoms, and intrusive thoughts (Arneson, 2015). These symptoms are often made worse by professional barriers to helping the trauma-impacted individual. In a school setting, this can include difficulties in getting services for students, poor family resources, inadequate self-care, and struggles with the day-in, day-out bureaucracy of education. Often confused with professional burnout, people suffering from compassion fatigue seldom dissociate from their feelings, losing the capacity to care. Instead, compassion fatigue can result in complete overwhelm by personal thoughts and emotions, making the job that much more difficult.

There are several ways educators and others involved in helping children impacted by trauma can prevent compassion fatigue. Begin with appropriate work-life balance. Maintain wellness activities, like healthy eating and sleep patterns, exercise, and mindfulness. Enlist the help of friends. Research demonstrates that social support helps mitigate the negative impact of stress (McGonigal, 2015). Be willing to feel whatever emotions surface as you help others. Dissociating from feelings can result in higher levels of stress. Develop a self-care plan that lists immediate and long-term care practices.

Ask for help and access available resources if you find yourself struggling to maintain your emotional regulation. Working with children impacted by trauma and toxic stress can be difficult. Their stories can be overwhelming. Don't downplay the impact you may feel. Being empathetic is one of the reasons you can help others.

Healing the Heart

Chapter 10 discussed the impact of defining oneself by one's traumas. Through the information and activities, you were given tools to help change your relationship with the trauma and help your children move forward. Specific attention was given to evidence-based strategies that help trauma-impacted children and adults rewrite the trauma story and change the impact of the trauma on daily functioning.

Heart-Centered Ideas

- The impact of trauma can permeate all aspects of a person's life—now and into the future.
- Post-traumatic growth is possible.
- Healing after trauma involves changing your thoughts about the trauma and its impact.
- Secondary trauma can happen as parents and other helpers support the healing of children. It needs to be understood in order to minimize its negative impact.

Healing Actions

- Think about post-traumatic growth. What growth have you noticed in you and/or your children? Write your answer in the space provided on Worksheet 4: My Journey Through Trauma (pp. 57–61).

- Thinking about gratitude and forgiveness, what is one thing you are grateful for with regard to trauma? Is there something or someone you are ready to forgive? Write your answers in the appropriate section of Worksheet 4.

Chapter 11
Through My Eyes

Conversations With Trauma-Impacted Children—A Middle School Focus Group

$\heartsuit$

I love running focus groups with students from elementary through high school. It is something I started back in 2010 when I wrote my first self-help book for kids, *101 Success Secrets for Gifted Kids*. Through the groups, I have met with hundreds of children asking questions about giftedness, anxiety, expectations, peer pressures, and even traumatic events.

In a recent focus group with students identified as gifted, one of the conversations wandered to community-based trauma, including school shootings, immigration policies in the border states, and violence. The following conversation was taken from part of that discussion. I include it because it spoke to the impact of community-based trauma, as well as ways to help students move forward.

Before I recount the actual interview, I wanted to share a few of the demographic details of the students who participated. The group consisted of seven students in seventh and eighth grades (four boys and three girls). Each student was identified as gifted by their school district. Ethnicity of the group consisted of White (2), Hispanic (4), and African American (1). No information was known regarding socioeconomic status or political affiliation. The students picked the community trauma topics, including the following interview about immigration.

This interview is not meant to make any political statement about the merits of the current immigration policy in the United States. The only goal of the interview was to explore the impact of the policies on children without judgment and based on the opinions of the children themselves. As with all of my focus groups, participants are not required to give their names, and I inform participants that any use of the interviews or stories involve by changing identifying information not necessary to the discussion. For that reason, the students are identified as Students 1 through 7 in the interview.

♡ ♡ ♡

Interviewer:	Thank you, again, for participating in the focus group. As we start this section of the group, I'd like to talk about the communities you live in and any difficulties you see within the community. What are some of the community experiences that you find potentially challenging?
Student 1:	Random acts of violence. Like the shooting that happened at some party last weekend.
Student 6:	Or school shootings.
Student 2:	I'm uncomfortable with the pot shops that are springing up everywhere.
Student 3:	For me, the biggest worry in my neighborhood is ICE.
Student 4:	Yeah. I worry about ICE raids all of the time.
Student 7:	Really? More than school shootings?
Student 3:	Definitely.
Interviewer:	Let's take a few of those worries one by one. What is the worry with immigration? Are you worried for your parents or other family members?
Student 3:	For me, I worry about my family. Even talking to you makes me worried that you will report something that will put my family in danger.
Student 4:	My teacher says that school is safe. And maybe that is true for me. But what about my family?

Through My Eyes—A Middle School Focus Group

Interviewer: I won't report anything related to immigration. Have any of you had experience with ICE raids?

Student 5: I have a cousin that was picked up and deported a year ago. And an aunt told us that her brother was taken outside of his church. Our family doesn't want to go anywhere anymore. I'm a citizen, so they let me come to school. But not everyone in my whole family is here legally. So, everyone worries all of the time.

Student 2: Yeah, we worry, too. It just isn't safe out there. It's something my parents talk about all of the time. And no matter what people tell me, I worry. A lot.

Interviewer: Is that true for most of you? Is this something that causes a lot of stress in your family?

(Several students nod.)

Student 1: I didn't know you guys think about that or that it's happened in your family. That's not right. I wish I could do something to help.

Student 6: Me too.

Interviewer: How does worrying about ICE affect those of you impacted by it? How often are you thinking or worrying?

Student 3: All of the time. Seriously. Every minute. My mom said I'm going to give myself heart problems because I worry so much.

Student 2: My parents have changed things at home because we had to take in my aunt. She's undocumented and afraid she'll be deported. So we protect her.

Student 5: Same here. I worry for my dad all of the time. Most days, I don't want to go to school. I feel like if I'm there, nothing will happen. When I do come, I can't really think about school, even though my mom tells me to just worry about my classes. It all feels unimportant, you know?

Student 4: I have this reoccurring dream that I'm being chased by ICE agents. They never catch me in my dreams, but I worry about it all of the time.

Interviewer: Is there anyone at school you can talk to about things?

Student 2: This isn't something you talk about with people outside of the family.

Student 5: My counselor is cool and all, but no one can really do anything about ICE, so I don't talk about it.

Student 7: I don't think people here think about the impact of the raids. Just like they don't really think about other stuff that happens to us outside of school. Everyone just expects us to be "normal" kids here at school—worry about grades, and friends, and that stuff. They don't have a clue what life is really like here.

Student 3: My teacher once asked me why I was sleeping in class and didn't complete my homework. I didn't feel like I could tell her it was because my uncle was just picked up by ICE and homework wasn't something I even thought about.

Interviewer: You mentioned that the adults at school don't understand the world you live in now. If you could tell your teachers, counselors, and the other school personnel anything, what would you want them to know?

Student 5: I'd want them to know that there are a lot of things happening at home these days. School isn't the only thing I think about—not even close. And while college seems like a great idea, I'm not sure it's realistic for me.

Student 7: I'd want my teachers to actually ask me what's going on and care about the answer. I mean, my teachers do ask sometimes, but it seems like it is in passing, like they don't really have the time to listen to my answer. I'm not sure they would really want the answer, anyway.

Student 1: Yeah, I feel the same way. Like if I told them all of the stuff I actually deal with daily, they'd freak out. Or get me or my family in trouble.

Student 3: I'd want them to understand the difficulties of living undocumented. I know my family chose this life. But to them, this wasn't a bad choice. What happened here is better than what happened where we come from, according to my dad. I wish somebody would understand that and stop making assumptions about what kind of people we are. We just want the chance for a good life. Worrying every day that my parents will be deported is hard.

Student 6: I may not worry about ICE raids like the others, but life isn't always easy, either. I wish teachers just remembered what it's like to deal with big, hard things. They have to know, right? They have to have experienced hard things at some point in their lives, right? So, why is it so hard for them to show compassion and understanding when we go through stuff? Most of the time I think they are assuming we are trying to play them, that we're lying about why we aren't ready for the test or whatever. I wish they would just assume I'm telling them the truth, that something big is happening and maybe I need some help.

Interviewer: How about the rest of you? Do you have anything to add?

Student 4: I think my teachers are pretty good. They don't really ask about my life outside of school, but I am okay with that. I don't want to share it, anyway. It's the office staff I struggle with. Like when they get on me because I'm late. They don't understand that I'm up every morning before 5 just so I can help with the house and my brothers and sisters before I go to school. They don't know that I have to get my younger sisters to childcare first. Or that my mom works two jobs and my dad is deployed most of the time. My teachers get it, so I don't understand why the office staff doesn't get it.

Student 2: I try to understand that my teachers and the other adults at school will never get what it is to be a kid today. Things are different. Harder. But I do wish they understood that we aren't lazy. That even when we sleep in class, or don't show up at all, or come but do nothing, there is always a reason. Maybe we are dealing with some tough home stuff. Maybe we are hungry or tired. Maybe we stayed up all night to play video games just to ignore our parents fighting. There is always more to what is happening than what they see.

Interviewer: We got a little off track from our conversation about immigration and trauma. Is there anything else about the long-term impact of worrying about immigration or being deported you'd like to share before we talk about other types of community trauma?

Student 2: The fear of ICE is real for me. It impacts what I think about the world. And yeah, some days I forget about it and I am just a kid. But that never lasts too long. Soon, something happens in our neighborhood, and the fear is back again.

Student 3: Same for me. I think most people don't think about the long-term impact of all of this on us, the kids. But imagine how you'd feel if you didn't know whether or not your parent would be there after you left school, or whether they'd be deported. How well would you do on your math test with that worry hanging around?

Student 5: I guess I just want more of what we said earlier—compassion and understanding. I don't want to be anything other than a normal kid. That's all any of us want, really. But we don't live "normal" lives. That's just a fact. I just need everyone to get that. When they hear about some big ICE raid or new conversation about deporting everyone, I hope they remember the impact to us, the kids.

This was just one of the many conversations around community trauma I've had with children. It provided insight as to the impact community issues have on the lives of our children, even when we think they are not impacted. Our current generations of kids are more aware of the world than we may realize. I hope you find this interview helpful as you deepen your understanding of the range of impact traumatic events can have on the lives of our youth.

The final section of *Healing the Heart* moves from strategies to survive trauma to thriving after the event. You will learn ways to redefine the trauma for both you and your children. You will also get answers to the most frequently asked questions I've received over the years.

Part IV

From Surviving to Thriving

The final section of *Healing the Heart* focuses on specific strategies and tips for living a full life, beyond the impact of trauma and toxic stress. The word *thrive* is often defined as meaning to flourish or prosper. This is precisely what this section sets out to do—support parents in helping children impacted by trauma move from merely processing through the traumatic events to flourishing.

Each chapter tackles a specific environment: home, school, and the larger world. Specific strategies are provided to help children reclaim their life, navigate challenging times, and redefine or discover their passions and purpose in the world. Additionally, each chapter features a "Frequent Asked Questions" section to tackle some of the more common wonderings from parents and educators around the world.

As the section ends, one last story of hope is included to illustrate how traumatic events can be redefined into pivotal moments of purpose.

Chapter 12

Thriving at Home

$\heartsuit$

As you make a move from merely surviving the traumatic events of your life to thriving, and helping your children do the same, it seems only appropriate to start with the home environment. Chapter 12 is about healing the family community, whether the traumatic events originated at home or elsewhere. Rebuilding family relationships, healing past wounds, and changing the future story of the family are vital to transcend the adverse experiences of the trauma.

Integrating the Trauma Story

As you and your children begin to recover and grow from the traumatic experience, you will start to want to revisit the story of your trauma. This usually doesn't happen in the early stages of processing, as the story itself may be too painful, often soliciting strong emotions that can retraumatize you or your children. Eventually, however, as you learn coping strategies and deal with the impact the trauma and toxic stress has had on you and/or your children, the need to analysis the story for errors and integrate the events into your memory may be necessary. This step is seldom accomplished without the help of trauma-trained mental health professionals. Additionally, it is not something to be attempted before the areas of safety, healthy relationship and boundary development, and social-emotional learning have been addressed. However, once these domains have begun to develop and heal, integrating the trauma story is a great way to move from surviving to thriving.

Often called trauma narration, integration of the story behind the trauma typically begins with writing down the traumatic event in detail. If many events have occurred, like when children are placed in the foster system or when a family has prolonged poverty exposure, it may be helpful to write a chronological timeline of events, as well as detailed accounts of the most impacting moments of that timeline.

It may take several weeks or therapy sessions to craft your trauma story. If you and your children are both receiving therapeutic services, you will likely go through trauma narration at different times and in individual sessions. Often there are intense emotions that accompany explorations of your trauma. It is crucial to have a repertoire of coping strategies to move through intense emotions and maintain internal safety without the risk of retraumatization (Cohen et al., 2017).

After the narrative has been crafted, your therapist will likely go through the story with you, discussing the details and looking for potential cognition errors. These are moments within the storyline in which your brain has potentially made inaccurate and/or unhelpful connections, creating unnecessary storylines. For example, if the traumatic events involve abuse, your child may believe they were the cause of the violence, deserving anything that happened to them. This would be an example of inaccurate recall. In this case, the therapist would work with the child's trauma narrative to correct that part of the story, placing blame for the abuse squarely on the abuser.

Another example of a cognition error could be recalling details that hyperbolize the impact of the trauma. For instance, a child may have experienced a traumatic death when they were very young. In the story, they recall their father getting into a car crash and dying before their fifth birthday. Because of the death, they may believe that they will never be truly happy as the death has left a deep emptiness inside they can never escape. Although this may have felt initially true, continuing with the story of never surviving grief or pain doesn't help them recover from the trauma. Integrating that story may involve rewriting that part of the story to say that initially, they felt as though they would never again feel joy. As time passes, however, they are beginning to heal. This is not only more likely accurate, but it also serves them better as the child moves toward growth and recovery.

As therapy continues, children and adults can learn how to talk about traumatic events without being overwhelmed by the experience or retraumatizing themselves. Role-plays can help individuals gain perspective and tap into their inner voice of wisdom to correct cognition errors. This is when deep healing begins, and people move into a new chapter, one not defined by the traumatic events or the initial impact of these events.

It is vital for families impacted by trauma to experience trauma narration, both individually and collectively. Just as individuals must learn to integrate and redefine the role of the trauma story within their lives, so does the family unit. With the help of a trained therapist, it is possible to heal the family and each member of the household.

Integrating trauma stories is messy, but rewarding, work. Through the process of rewriting your trauma story, you can begin to experience more joy and fulfillment in life. Tip Sheet 13: Rewriting My Story gives some suggestions for working on your trauma narrative. Remember that this work is best accomplished with the help of trauma-trained mental health professionals.

Healing the Family

As discussed in Part III, rebuilding healthy relationships and establishing close connections is essential for post-traumatic growth. Working on the trauma narrations as a family system is one way to heal the family. Correcting faulty thinking around the family dynamic, as well as memory inaccuracies about the trauma, is a way the family can begin to heal.

Sometimes, however, healing the relationships between parents or other family members and the children is not possible. This is particularly true if the parents or other family members perpetrated the trauma.

Tip Sheet 13

Rewriting My Story

---

o Write down what happened during the traumatic event. This is your origin story. Remember that a good story has a beginning, a middle, and an end. Your story does too. Write it all down.
o Answer the following questions about the story:
  • What does the story make you think about?
  • What beliefs did you form about the world as a result of the experience?
  • Can you identify places in your story where your thinking may be (a) inaccurate or (b) unhelpful? How can you correct your story to correct your thinking?
  • What lessons did you learn from your story?
  • What strengths do you see within *you* in the story?
  • How can you use these strengths to help you grow from your experience?

Although reconciliation may not always be possible between the people involved in the incident, individuals can move forward and integrate their unique trauma stories.

I once worked with a college student who had experienced sexual abuse from a parent. Although she was never on speaking terms with the parent, she was able to process through her trauma story and reconcile the events in her mind. She switched from believing that she was the cause of the abuse ("I was punished for being a girl.") to understanding that she did not make her father molest her, and being a girl did not mean she should be raped. She also moved from believing she could never have a healthy relationship ("I only know how to be with abusers. I don't think I'll ever know how to be in a healthy relationship.") to realizing she could choose healthy relationships. It was challenging for her to learn to set healthy boundaries and assert her needs, but it was possible. She could learn to experience healthy relationships and expect healthy behavior from her significant other.

When healing the family of origin is not possible, remember that it is still possible to experience the community of family. In that community, you are seen, heard, and valued as part of the group. You can experience safety, connect with others, and heal the neurobiological fragmentation that occurred as a result of the trauma. Creating a sense of belonging within another group can happen within a school setting, through extracurricular activities, within areas of similar interest, and even with individual people. For many children impacted by trauma, this type of connection is found with other caring adults, like educators and support staff.

Looking Ahead

Many children impacted by trauma struggle to see a life beyond the traumatic events that occurred. As the narrative begins to be rewritten, children can imagine a future beyond the trauma they experienced. They can dream of a life in which they are happy and safe. It is vital at this stage to help children identify possible future goals, areas of interest or purpose, and ways to dream of future plans. It is equally important to teach children how to achieve these goals and act on their dreams.

Begin with goal setting. Teach children to plan for obstacles and develop a growth mindset. Develop self-motivation skills in your children. These skills will enable children to achieve more than they believed possible before they began to integrate their trauma stories. Tip Sheet 14: Looking Toward the Future lists several strategies to help children move past the traumatic events and set and achieve their goals.

Frequently Asked Questions:
Thriving at Home

For the past several years, numerous questions have come up during parent coaching and workshop settings around the topic of trauma. I wanted to include several of the questions and answers here in the hopes that it could answer some of the continued questions you have at this point. The following five questions deal specifically with parents and the

Tip Sheet 14

Looking Toward the Future

Use the following tips to help your child practice writing goals and thinking about the future.

- Set a goal you'd like to achieve. Think about it in measurable terms.
  - Example: "I would like to learn mindfulness."

- Use the following steps to write a goal:
  - Set a reasonable timeframe for the goal (e.g., "by next week").
  - Clearly and specifically indicate what you will do (e.g., "I will try three new ways to practice mindfulness.").
  - Indicate how you will do it (e.g., "by picking one the night before, and doing it before dinner").
  - Complete writing the goal: "By next week, I will try three new ways to practice mindfulness by picking one the night before, and doing the activity before dinner."

- What kind of problems or barriers might arise?
  - Example: "(1) I may forget to do it; (2) it may be weird doing it; (3) my mom might ask me why I'm doing it."

- Write a plan for each potential barrier.
  - Example: "(1) I will set a reminder on my phone each night so I don't forget to do the activity. (2) I know it will feel weird, but I want to do this to help get better at managing my stress. So I will just remind myself everyday why I am doing this. (3) I will tell my mom about mindfulness and why I want to do it. No matter what she suggests, this is my decision, so I am going to follow through. I really want my mom to be supportive, so I will tell her why it is so important to me."

- What do you want to feel as a result of achieving your goal?
  - Example: "I want to feel pride for completing my goal and thankful for having more options to manage my stress."

home setting. I've also included practical tips and strategies throughout the section to assist with the answers.

Q: My child is very shy and hesitant to talk about the traumatic event with anyone. How can I help her if she won't talk about it?

A: First, understand that most people, whether children or adults, are reluctant to talk about their trauma stories. I don't recommend pushing your child to discuss things they are not ready to discuss, unless it is with the assistance of a mental health professional. That said, you don't need to openly discuss the specifics of the traumatic events to help a child heal and move forward. You simply need to be there for your child. Focus on the relationship with your child or children. Speak openly about your feelings and thoughts, as well as theirs. As questions surface, answer them—no matter how difficult it may be for you. The important thing is to provide the space for your children to begin to deal with whatever emotions they may have as a result of the traumatic events. By focusing on the relationships between you and your children, and remaining open to wherever the conversations meander, you are creating an environment of trust and safety necessary for healing.

Tip Sheet 15: Talking About Trauma has specific strategies if your child or children decide to talk about their trauma stories with you directly. These tips can help you navigate the conversation and communicate the security your family may need. Talking about the trauma may be difficult, especially if the events involved you as well. There is no perfect way for the conversation to unfold. Just remain focused on honest communication, clear emotional reactions, and strengthening your relationships.

Q: I'm afraid that if people find out about the traumatic things we've been through, they are going to make a lot of judgments about me and my children. How can I help people see past the story and not define my children by the things that have happened to them?

Tip Sheet 15

Talking About Trauma

When a child appears ready to talk about their trauma story, use the following tips to help support them.

- Invite the child to talk about the traumatic events.
- Reassure the child that they are currently safe. Remind them that they can grow past the impact the trauma may have had on them.
- Use active listening strategies. Ask for clarification as needed.
- Listen to the child with a goal of understanding them. Resist the urge to "fix" anything.
- Encourage the child to talk about and show emotions.
- Share your emotions.
- Focus on the positive as much as possible, without ignoring hard emotions.
- Encourage productive action.
- Get support and help as needed.

A: I would love to be able to say that this will never happen. Unfortunately, you and I both know that isn't how the world works. People do make assumptions about trauma and adverse childhood experiences. They make assumptions about abuse, mental health, poverty, and so much more. But here's the thing—it actually doesn't matter what other people think. It matters what you and your family think.

Let me explain that a bit more. Although dealing with other people's judgments and biases is difficult, there is little you can directly do to change their beliefs or even recognize when they are being biased. Instead of focusing your energies there, I would focus on strengthening you and your children's beliefs about your situation and the traumatic events you have endured. Be willing to openly talk about the events within the family—without guilt and without shame. I know I am asking a lot. It is a normal part of recovery to blame yourself for whatever horrible things you and your children have experienced, even if the events were beyond your control. This is even more true if you hold some responsibility for the events. Getting stuck in the shame-blame game doesn't help your children, however. Nor does it help you.

You may need help from a mental health professional to move past your strong emotional reactions to the difficult events you've experienced. Your children may need help, as well. This is fine. Get the support all of you need. You must all forgive yourselves for the events and move past defining yourself by them.

Worksheet 8: Strength of My Trauma is an activity you and your children can use to help redefine the impact of your trauma stories. Through the questions, you can rewrite this part of your lives and begin to find the upside of the experiences. When you and your children can redefine things in this way, you begin to not only change your inner mindsets, but also challenge the biases and judgments of others. Even if others refuse to change their opinions of you, it doesn't matter; you are able to move forward without being negatively impacted by others.

Q: Most days I am barely able to function because of what happened. How do I help my child when I am barely holding on?

A: Moving forward after extreme events is more than a little difficult. Moving forward with the responsibility of caring for another person can be even more difficult. You must get support as you go through the process of healing. Friends, family members, mental health professionals, the school and other community agencies—allow others to form your supportive circle and help you as you move through the cycle of grief and begin to heal. This isn't the time to be ashamed or embarrassed. This is the time to accept the help when you need it. Take respites from your caregiving responsibilities for a night. Allow a neighbor to bring over dinner. Say "yes" when a teacher offers to help your children with their work. This is support you may need during your healing process.

Use Tip Sheet 16: Practicing Self-Care anytime you feel yourself getting overwhelmed and struggling to care for others.

Worksheet 8
Strength of My Trauma

Directions: Think about the traumatic event you or your child experienced. Using the guiding questions, complete the worksheet.

Traumatic Event *What happened?*	Impact *How were you affected? Think of all of the ways.*	Strengths Used *Identify the different character strengths you used to survive the event.*

Traumatic Event What happened?	Impact How were you affected? Think of all of the ways.	Strengths Used Identify the different character strengths you used to survive the event.

Tip Sheet 16
Practicing Self-Care

- Develop and use a mindfulness practice.
- Develop and use a forgiveness practice.
- Develop and use a gratitude practice.
- Develop and use healthy lifestyle habits, including healthy food choices, adequate amounts of high-quality sleep, and adequate exercise.
- Forgo passive, mind-numbing activities (e.g., watching television) and go outside for a walk instead.
- Cultivate friendships and social connections.
- Develop and practice optimism.

The events you and your children have experienced have a lasting impact on all of you. You would not expect your children to simply "get over things," right? Don't expect yourself to, either. Take the time you need to take in order to heal. And get help for you and your children throughout the process.

Q: My spouse thinks most of this "trauma stuff" is why our society has become too weak and unable to cope with normal life. How can I help my spouse understand this information and help our child who clearly struggles?

A: Many people struggle to understand the deep impact of trauma on our minds and bodies. Indeed, there are people who believe that the best way to deal with adversity is to "suck it up and move forward." By this point of the book, however, you have seen the research and understand why it is neither healthy nor appropriate to simply ignore the emotional upheaval that some people feel when experiencing trauma. The brain and body do change as a result of the stress caused by adverse experiences. This change can be negative. If there are people in your life, like your spouse or other family members, who don't believe in the harmful effects of trauma, you can try to educate them with the current research. Try to have an open conversation about your concerns for your children or yourself. Explain what you have learned from this book or other sources.

The truth is, there is nothing in this book—no strategy or suggestion—that will make you or your children less functional. Recognizing your trauma story and moving from a victim to survivor mindset won't reduce your resilience. Focusing on reframing experiences from negative to positive won't result in a weaker or less adaptive mindset. All of the tips, strategies, and activities were included specifically because they will strengthen your grit, increase resiliency, and improve social-emotional health—all good things.

Tip Sheet 17: My Resiliency Strategies reviews many of the strategies referenced throughout the book alongside the skills they develop. Show this to anyone who questions why you are reading this book or focusing on healing from your difficult experiences. They will soon see that, even though they may not understand or agree with your beliefs about trauma, the things you are doing to help yourself and your children will do nothing but improve the household resiliency and make all of you more able to adapt to whatever the future may hold—all good things.

Q: I've read that people who have four or more ACEs experience very bad health outcomes. Is it really possible to change this?

A: The research around adverse childhood experiences (ACEs) is clear—the higher your ACE score, the more negative your potential health outcomes. Notice I said potential. This is because nothing with our bodies involves forgone conclusions. Yes, children whose ACE score is above 4 are more likely to experience heart problems, potential diabetes, and more. But this is assuming no intervention. As children learn to understand their internal stress stories related to the adverse experience, they can learn to rewrite that story. They can develop improved social-emotional skills and change their DNA, liter-

---

Tip Sheet 17

My Resiliency Strategies

- Teach and practice optimism.
- Use books and media to learn about growth mindset and perseverance.
- Practice cognitive flexibility through creativity exercises. Try using some of the "spontaneous" activities from Odyssey of the Mind to start.
- Develop and practice mindfulness activities.
- Use an emotion wheel to develop emotional literacy.

Note. Adapted from Fonseca, 2019.

---

ally. This can change how their body responds to the toxic stress and completely change their health outcomes.

Remember the stress research highlighted in Chapter 3. What we think about stress matters. A lot. The same is true for our trauma experiences. The important thing is to help our children redefine stress, adversity, and the trauma itself. This doesn't mean denying what occurred. On the contrary, it means clarifying what happened and making different meaning of it—moving from a deficit mindset (how you were victimized by the events) to a strengths mindset (identifying the strengths you gained as a result of the events). It is from the latter mindset that your children can begin to change the potential negative health outcomes—both physical and psychological.

Healing the Heart

Part IV is all about flourishing. In Chapter 12, you deepened your ability to integrate the trauma story into your life and help your children do the same. The FAQ section reviewed several questions you may have still had about trauma and supporting your children at home.

Heart-Centered Ideas

- Healing the family and moving forward is possible, no matter what the trauma impact has been.
- Integrating the trauma story into one's life, and not ignoring the impact, is an important aspect of moving forward.
- There are times when you or your children may be emotionally triggered and the trauma story reignited. Learning what to do when this occurs is an important aspect of healing.

Healing Actions

- Review the progress you have made thus far. What do you notice about you or your children's relationship with the trauma? Use Worksheet 4: My Journey Through Trauma (pp. 57–61) to write down your thoughts.
- Determine one to two areas you would like to continue to work through. What is the goal for these areas? How can you achieve them? Use Worksheet 4 to write down your thoughts.

Chapter 13
Thriving at School

♡

Beginning the healing process at home is essential, but thriving within the school environment is also crucial. This could be particularly necessary if the traumatic events involved the educational setting, as in the case of bullying or school violence. Repairing relationships with adults and peers, as well as redefining what the educational environment means to trauma-impacted children, are essential aspects of learning to thrive within the school community. Chapter 13 focuses on helping educators to partner in the healing process of children, regardless of where or how the traumatic events occurred. Parents will find this chapter informative, and it will provide various conversation starters if you need to have difficult discussions with your children's educators.

The Trauma-Informed School

By now, you understand the significant impact of trauma and toxic stress on both adults and children. You are trauma-informed. Helping the educational environment become trauma-informed or trauma-sensitive means consideration within the system is given to the impact traumatic events have on students and families. It shifts the conversation from "What is wrong with you?" to "What may have happened to you?" (The National Child Traumatic Stress Network, 2018). Trauma-informed care focuses on avoiding retraumatization, understands that many concerning behaviors initially began as coping strategies, and understands each trauma-impacted person within their unique social and cultural context (Arneson, 2015).

Hodas (2006) conceptualized three core concepts within a model of trauma-informed care: understanding, commitment, and practice. In this model, understanding refers to primary education around trauma—the causes, prevalence, and impact—and how to serve those impacted. The model further defines the need to understand self-directed and person-centered approaches to trauma treatment that are strengths-oriented and collaborative.

The commitment concept of the model refers to the need to have partnerships within the trauma-informed system that involve leadership and ensure that all members of the system receive adequate training and support to help those impacted by trauma. Practices refer specifically to evidence-based strategies that build upon the strengths of the individual, are strengths-based, and incorporate screening methods to identify people within the system who may need support (Hodas, 2006).

Walkley and Cox (2013), drawing on the "Ten Principles of Compassionate Schools" (Washington State Office of Superintendent of Public Instruction, 2011), highlighted several ways schools can be more trauma-informed. Consistent with Hodas's (2006) work, creating understanding through educating school personnel, utilizing evidence-based practices rooted in a strengths approach, and developing systems and structures that promote safe learning environments were all identified as necessary in the trauma-informed school.

Additional ways schools can support students impacted by trauma and toxic stress can be found on Tip Sheet 20: Becoming Trauma-Informed later in this chapter.

More Than Their Stories

One of the most important ways schools can support trauma-impacted children is by seeing beyond the trauma students may bring to school. This idea of being person-centered involves the language educators use when discussing students, as well as the way the instructional staff sees students. Using person-first language means shifting from defining students by their difficulties (i.e., special education students, problem behavior children, disruptive students) to person-oriented language (students with exceptional needs, children with behavior challenges, students who struggle with behavior management). The shift in style helps to remind all members of the educational community that a student is, first and foremost, a person. The difficulties experienced by the students do not define them.

Utilizing person-first language also helps remind everyone that the difficulties are not necessarily permanent or fixed. Students can move past their experiences with trauma and reintegrate their trauma stories. They can learn coping strategies and social-emotional learning skills. They can change.

Focusing on individual students and not the specific details of their traumatic experiences also helps educators avoid the trap of "Who has the biggest trauma?" that can occasionally occur. When instructional staff fall into this trap, assumptions about the impact of trauma are made based on perceptions of the staff, not the actual effect of the traumatic events on an individual. As discussed in Chapter 6, this type of thinking is neither culturally sensitive nor trauma-informed. Nor is it particularly helpful to students. As educators begin to see students first, they create the opportunity to see students' strengths, as well as their capacity to maximize their potential. The shift in thinking allows for more significant opportunities for students within the educational system. At this point, the school setting becomes a support for students as they move from recovery into post-traumatic growth.

Supporting All Students to Thrive

In a landmark report by the Aspen Institute National Commission on Social, Emotional, and Academic Development (2018), *From a Nation at Risk to a Nation at Hope*, the commission highlighted several ways that schools can support the learning and social-emotional development of all students. The report cites significant bodies of research across a variety of scientific disciplines that indicate the connection between the social, emotional, and cognitive aspects of learning. Six critical recommendations for ways schools can support the health and development of students are provided, including:

1. creating a vision for educating and support the whole child, including social, emotional, and academic domains;
2. ensuring safe and supportive learning environments for all students;
3. embedding social, emotional, and cognitive skills into all areas of academic instruction;
4. increasing adult understanding of child development and learning;
5. aligning community resources to address the needs of the whole child; and
6. closely connecting research to practice.

When looked at more closely, each of the recommendations aligns with the best practices for developing trauma-informed systems and compassionate schools. By focusing on the recommendations from the report, schools can help support children impacted by traumatic events move past their trauma and toxic stress, and heal.

Frequently Asked Questions: Thriving at School

This chapter focuses on ways to transform the school setting into being trauma-sensitive and trauma-informed. The following questions represent many of the common questions I receive when providing educator trainings or during online discussions.

Q: What is the first step in helping a student who is completely stuck in their trauma story?

A: Students often demonstrate difficult behaviors due to the impact of trauma. When a child yells or runs from the class, it may relate to the specific trauma that the student has experienced and how that event is continuing to impact their functioning. When a student has been working through the impact of trauma, they may be willing to adjust behavior easily. However, if the student has not yet begun working through the impact of their experiences, or isn't even aware of the connection between their behavior and the experiences, it may be difficult for educators to know how to best support and help. Begin with the assumption that all behavior—good and not-so-good—occurs as a way to communicate something. Also assume that when children know how to respond differently, they do. This means that difficult behaviors are always communicating something, and the child chooses this particular behavior because, for now, it is the only way they can easily express whatever they are trying to express.

With all of that in mind, there are several things you can do to help support a student who is struggling with their behaviors, regardless of how stuck they are in their trauma stories. First, think safety. When students are impacted by trauma, their world feels unsafe most of the time. Creating and maintaining safe environments are a key to helping students. Next, stay calm and help orient the student to the present moment and time. Often, trauma-impacted students fall in and out of the traumatic events, getting triggered and feeling like they are back in the moment of the event. Focus on calming the student without feeding the behavior. If the student needs a break, give them one. Limit your language and proximity, while reminding the student of the strategies they have learned to manage behavior (assuming there has been some practice with using coping skills).

Tip Sheet 18: Deescalating Students includes many more ideas for helping students calm and regain control over their behavior when they appear locked in their trauma stories. Remember to reestablish both safety and positive relationships with students after the behavior escalation. This will remind students that they are not their trauma and that you see beyond the intense behaviors.

Q: How can we really help students when we never know their stories? Is there a way to help if you don't actually know what happened and what their triggers are?

A: Educators rarely know when a student has experienced significant trauma or when the behaviors they see a child exhibiting are related to trauma. Fortunately, you don't need to know the specific traumas a student has experienced in order to render help and support. You just need to be willing to assume that there is always a story of some sort behind behavior, and often that story includes traumatic events. Supporting students with trauma begins with an understanding that everyone is impacted by the lives they have lived. The impact of the various experiences can be a source of pain and a source of strength. For students, adopting a mindset of "What may have happened to you that has resulted in your behaviors and thinking?" is an excellent way to ensure that you are approaching the situation from a trauma-informed position. Focusing on establishing safety, creating predictable routines and responses, and remaining focused on cultivating positive relationships with your students are specific ways you can support those students who may be impacted by trauma and toxic stress. Partnering with the mental health support staff on your campus to help the students develop coping strategies and begin to heal the negative impact of the trauma also helps to support the students. Refer to Table 8 for additional ways you can support your trauma-impacted students.

Tip Sheet 18

Deescalating Students

Try the following strategies to help students deescalate when triggered.

Before a Problem Occurs

o Develop positive teacher-student relationships.
o Understand the impact of trauma and toxic stress.
o Establish clear expectations and consequences.
o Explicitly teach prosocial skills.
o Teach social problem-solving and conflict resolution skills.
o Provide high levels of positive performance feedback.
o Pick and choose your battles.

During a Crisis

o Reduce language use.
o Switch from terminating to initiating commands.
o Resist the urge to engage in a verbal sparring match with the student.
o Provide minimal eye contact and attention until the student begins to show compliance.
o Don't force task/command compliance.
o Allow time and space to cool down.
o When making commands, (1) increase wait time, (2) give one direction at a time, (3) use short, direct language, and (4) give only as many commands as absolutely necessary.

After the Crisis

o Review expectations and consequences.
o Reaffirm and rebuild relationships.
o Reconcile harm and work with the student to do the same.
o Rebuild the classroom community.

Table 8
Creating a Network of Support

Role	Ways to Support Students Impacted by Trauma
Teacher and classroom support staff	• Establish safety within classroom. • Build positive connections. • Teach and model SEL skills. • Provide consistency and predictability. • Provide opportunities for student agency.
Other school staff	• Establish safety within school. • Build positive connections. • Model SEL skills. • Provide consistency and predictability. • Provide opportunities for student agency.
Administration	• Establish safety within school. • Build positive connections. • Model SEL skill development. • Establish restorative process to address behavior. • Provide consistency and predictability. • Provide opportunities for student agency. • Connect student to potential resources and support.
Mental health staff	• Explicitly teach SEL and related skills. • Address mental health concerns. • Help establish safety and positive connections. • Provide mental health first aid as necessary. • Link to community resources. • Progress monitor skill acquisition and generalization.

Q: What is the best way to deal with trauma in a group setting so that other children don't engage in bullying or gossipy behaviors?

A: As more and more teachers engage in community circles and classroom meetings, I have received more and more questions about dealing with trauma within a circle. I'd like to start by saying that the negative impact of trauma can show up at any time—in the behavior of the student, in comments made in response to "deeper" questions within the circle, and at other times. As you are setting up your community circles, remember to set up expectations, or norms, for the circles. Remind students that the point of the circle is to build a sense of community and deepen each others' knowledge and appreciation for the various lives lived by the students. The increased social awareness created by community circles can function as a protection factor for those who have experienced difficult events. Should inappropriate behavior—including bullying or belittling behavior—occur, address it within the circle and with the individual student immediately. By staying focused on teaching and acknowledging expected behaviors, as well as slowly building the trust within the community circle, you can help ensure that all members of the classroom community feel safe and respected.

Tip Sheet 19: Strategies for Successful Circles can provide additional ways to successfully run community circles without the potential for harming your students impacted by trauma.

Q: It seems like every child is negatively impacted by traumatic events today. What is the best way to ensure teachers are trained in trauma-informed practices sooner rather than later?

A: Trauma-informed training is vital for educators. As the research into the impact of trauma and toxic stress has increased, so has the need for educator training. Fortunately, there are many sources of training in this area. View trauma training for educators not as a separate thing to attend and think about, but rather as being linked to the overall framework the school and district use to address school climate and culture. "Trauma-informed" is a lens with which everything related to conditions and skills for learning is approached. In this way, the training about the impact of adverse childhood experiences, toxic stress, and what schools can do to support students impacted by trauma is not separate from the other supports being offered (i.e., Positive Behavior Intervention and Supports [PBIS], or Multi-Tiered Systems of Support [MTSS]). Rather, this training is an integrated part of everything the school does to increase safety and support the whole student.

Tip Sheet 19

Strategies for Successful Circles

- ○ Establish norms and expectations for circle behavior.
- ○ Acknowledge and correct behaviors quickly.
- ○ Start with "safe" questions.
- ○ Watch for trauma triggers.
- ○ Participate alongside students.

Note. Adapted from Fonseca, 2019.

The strategies listed on Tip Sheet 20: Becoming Trauma-Informed can help a district or school ensure that the systems and structures, including professional learning for educators, are embedded into the overall functioning of the educational system.

Q: *It seems like the strategies for supporting students impacted by trauma really benefit all students and should just be implemented universally. What additional strategies are needed specifically for students known to be impacted by trauma?*

A: Yes, strategies including creating safe spaces, building positive relationships, and developing predictable routines and responses are good for all students. They form a universal, trauma-informed foundation for all students that communicates safety. These strategies may be enough to support many of the students negatively impacted by adverse childhood experiences or other traumatic events. But what about students who need something more? What can be done specifically for those students?

Students who require additional support due to trauma and the impact of toxic stress may need specific coping strategies for managing their toxic stress. Instruction and practice of these coping skills can be done in a small group or individ-

Tip Sheet 20

Becoming Trauma-Informed

The following are guidelines to establish system-wide trauma-informed practices:
- o Begin with a district commitment to establishing a trauma-informed approach to supporting children.
- o Create a written policy reflecting a trauma-informed approach.
- o Invite stakeholders, including those impacted by trauma, to participate in the development of universal systems to support trauma-impacted youth.
- o Collaborate with community partners.
- o Embed trauma-informed practices into a tiered system of support for all students (e.g., MTSS).
- o Include evidence-based interventions to address children impacted by traumatic events within the tiered system of support. Train all stakeholders on the application of the interventions.
- o Develop effective progress and fidelity measures to track the impact of interventions.

Note. Adapted from Substance Abuse and Mental Health Services Administration, 2014.

ually, depending on the specific needs of the student and the intensity of that need. Tip Sheet 21: Specific Interventions for Trauma-Impacted Youth includes a list and brief descriptions of interventions for use with students in small groups or one-on-one counseling sessions. Training the classroom staff on the coping strategies and how to support their use is critical to help students use the coping strategies within all educational settings.

> ## Tip Sheet 21
> ### *Specific Interventions for Trauma-Impacted Youth*
>
> ○ Begin with a strong foundation of support:
>   - safety,
>   - positive adult-student relationships,
>   - clear expectations and consequences,
>   - predictability and consistency,
>   - SEL skill development, and
>   - opportunities for student voice and choice.
>
> ○ Keep emotional reactivity in check.
> ○ Revisit self-regulation skills with students often.
> ○ Build a positive class community.
> ○ Warn students of potential changes.
> ○ Focus on developing emotional literacy.
> ○ Teach and practice conflict resolution and social problem-solving skills.
> ○ Teach and practice organizational skills.
> ○ Teach and practice coping strategies.
> ○ Connect with students on a personal level.
> ○ Focus on successes while addresses areas of growth.

Healing the Heart

Chapter 13 shifted the focus from home to school and tackled the prospect of helping to support trauma-impacted youth achieve their life goals. The chapter provided strategies to help educators see beyond the trauma while still supporting the students' continued growth. In the FAQ section, questions related to supporting EQ and academic performance, secondary trauma for educators, and being a trauma-informed school were addressed.

Heart-Centered Ideas

- The best way to support children and families impacted by trauma is to become a trauma-informed school and use a trauma-informed lens when developing systems of support.
- Staff commonly experience secondary trauma and have primary trauma stories triggered by students. Providing educators information and support for both is a key to the successful implementation of trauma-informed practices.
- Integrating passion and purpose, as well as relationships and community, into the educational setting is crucial, as they are vital components of 21st-century schools.

Healing Actions

- Take a moment to review the tip sheets, as well as the FAQs. What questions do you still have? Use the space provided on Worksheet 4: My Journey Through Trauma (pp. 57–61) to write down your thoughts.
- Develop an action plan for how you'd like to bring this information into your educational setting. Use Worksheet 4 to write down your plan.

Chapter 14
Thriving in the World

♡

Our children live in more than the environments of home and school. They also exist in the greater community of the shared human experience. Thriving in the world involves finding pockets of connection and safety in the community, and using our traumatic stories to help others. Making this transition—beginning the process of reframing traumatic experiences into sources of strength—takes time. This chapter of *Healing the Heart* focuses on ways to turn painful stories of adversity and trauma into inspiring stories of hope and change for the world.

The Trauma-Informed Community

Just as schools benefit from a trauma-informed approach, creating environments that better support students, families, and staff impacted by trauma and toxic stress, so do other community agencies. The more that the institutions of society—medical, social, financial, corporate, faith, and criminal justice—can incorporate trauma-informed care components into day-to-day activities, the more these same institutions can collectively change the face of trauma and toxic stress (Arneson, 2015).

Consider the current societal inequities resulting from trauma. Children living in poverty have the most significant risk of exposure to traumatic events, both in the home and within the community (St. Andrews, 2013). Groups traditionally marginalized in society, including minorities, LGBTQ youth and adults, people with mental illness and physical disabilities, and the homeless, are at significant risk for exposure to ACEs (U.S. Department of Justice, 2012). Children exposed to ACEs are at significantly higher risk of incarceration (Children's Defense Fund, 2009), residential placements (Sedlak & McPherson, 2010), and severe substance abuse problems (The National Child Traumatic Stress Network, 2008b). Traumatic experiences impact more than children and families. The impact on the entire community is significant. By utilizing a trauma-informed approach, communities can begin to break cycles of abuse and violence, heal, and thrive post-trauma.

The Substance Abuse and Mental Health Services Administration (SAMHSA, 2014) has developed six critical ideas for implementing a trauma-informed approach in communities. The principles focus on linking services to recovery and resilience for families impacted by traumatic events. The key ideas include:

1. physical and psychological safety;
2. maintaining organizational transparency in order to foster trust with clients, families, staff, and throughout the organization;
3. peer support to promote healing and growth;
4. collaboration between all stakeholders and clients;
5. empowerment and agency, including voice and choice, to build self-advocacy skills; and
6. cultural sensitivity to address issues of bias and move past stereotypes.

By utilizing these six fundamental principles, organizations within communities will be able to support the needs of children and families fully. Collectively, whole communities can experience post-traumatic recovery, healing, and growth.

Becoming an Agent of Healing

One of the most potent ways to transcend recovery and thrive is to share your integrated trauma story. Through your experience, others can form a picture of what the world looks like post-trauma. Many survivors of trauma give back to the community through their stories, becoming peer supporters, and supporting agencies that focus on helping children and families impacted by trauma.

As you or your children recover from the traumatic experience, integrate the trauma narratives, and experience life beyond the stressful events, a natural urge to help others may develop. Share your story. Show others that it is possible to thrive after trauma. Many nonprofit organizations, inspirational speakers, and educational consultants have found ways to transform their experience from a source of pain to a tool of inspiration. You can do the same if you feel called to do so.

Trauma as a Strength

One of the first ways to use your experience as a tool of inspiration is to identify the character strengths you have used and/or gained from the traumatic events you survived. Think about all of the ways trauma has helped you cultivate your strengths. What did you learn? How did you overcome adversity? How are you now helping others? As you contemplate these questions, refer to Worksheet 8: Strength of My Trauma (p. 140). Is there anything you need to add? Take a few minutes and add to the information on the worksheet.

You and your children are more than your experiences with trauma. The toxic stress that once defined how your brain functioned need not limit your responses forever. You can change how you respond to adversity. You can deepen your resilience, grow, and thrive.

Frequently Asked Questions: Thriving in the World

Every time I conduct a trauma workshop, I am asked about ways people can positively impact the larger community and help others understand the role of trauma and toxic stress. I've collected a few of the more common questions for this section and focus on how to help others understand and support those who are trauma-impacted.

Q: It seems like everyone is impacted by trauma today. Is it really that prevalent, or are people just being overly sensitive?

A: Adverse childhood experiences are far more common than ever realized—that is one of the major findings of the original Felitti et al. (1998) research. As more research is conducted in the area of trauma, the field is beginning to realize that the impact of trauma is wide and significant. This is not to say that all humans have experienced traumatic events at a large enough scale to negatively impact mental and physical functioning. But a large percentage of the population has been impacted by traumatic events to some degree. Not only have large numbers of people experienced traumatic events, but also the understanding of the impact of trauma has increased significantly. As a result, people are talking about it more often and at a greater depth.

Further, there is increasing research suggesting that both iGen and Generation Alpha are experiencing a decline in self-esteem and resilience (Twenge & Campbell, 2018) and an increase in depression and anxiety (Twenge et al., 2018). The declines are largely correlated to increases in technology use and decreases in social-emotional skill development and have resulted in a reduction of people's capacity to cope with stress in general, let alone cope with toxic levels of stress. These converging factors—high exposure to traumatic events, increased awareness of the impact of trauma and toxic stress on the brain and body, and decreased capacity to cope with adverse experiences—have resulted in the appearance of super-sensitivity to trauma.

I don't believe people are experiencing more trauma, necessarily, although one could easily argue that life is getting increasingly more difficult at times. People are, however, more aware of the impact of the trauma. People have become more sensitive to stress and have grown less tolerant of its impact. And people struggle with coping skills, often turning to technology and other distractions without building their own internal coping mechanisms. Tip Sheet 22: Coping With Stress provides practical strategies for you and your child to begin to increase your ability to manage stressful events.

Q: There are a lot of conversations these days about trigger warnings and not retraumatizing people. What is the best way to have conversations about trauma without feeling like you are always walking on eggshells, hyperaware about others' feelings?

A: One of the consequences of our increased awareness of the impact of trauma on the brain and overall mental health is a realization around traumatization and the need to respect the variance of tolerance for triggering topics related to trauma. Although I completely agree that it is important to respect each other's trigger tolerance and potential for retraumatization, I also believe in the necessity of increasing individual stress tolerance and reframing trauma stories away from the negative and toward the positive. When you are in the early stages of healing from your trauma, this may seem impossible—how can you possibly view trauma as a positive? But reframing is critical in order to function within the world and move from surviving to thriving.

Talking about trauma normalizes the experience. It doesn't discount individual experiences around traumatic events, but it does say, "Many of us experience trauma, and we are all here to support one another." In order to best talk about trauma and the impact of toxic stress, be open about what your topics cover. If

Tip Sheet 22

Coping With Stress

Try these activities to help manage your stress.

- Take a deep breath.
- Stretch your arms and legs.
- Smile and laugh.
- Think of three things you are thankful for.
- Take a coloring break.
- Take a walk outside.
- Clean and declutter your room.
- Count to five—slowly.
- Talk with your parents or a counselor.
- Journal.
- Think of three things that bring you joy.
- Brush your pet's fur.
- Read.
- Call a friend.
- Practice mindful breathing.
- Picture someone doing something nice for you.

you are discussing potentially triggering topics, state that at the start. Give options for what your children (or students) should do if they feel an emotional wave surface. Teach breathing and journaling techniques. If you struggle with the regulation of your emotions in response to trauma, focus on improving that first. The more you are able to manage your emotions, the more you can provide an example of how to manage discussions around trauma.

Note that I am not suggesting a nonemotional stance. On the contrary, I strongly recommend remaining emotionally connected to the topic. If this means your emotions will surface, that is fine. But learn how to regulate those emotions so that you are not in distress by them. Children need to see how adults successfully manage strong emotions. This modeling provides hope to children who may struggle with tolerating their strong emotions, even criticizing themselves for experiencing strong feelings.

Q: I am always hearing that kids are less resilient today. How do we actually strengthen kids' abilities to cope if we are always coddling every fear?

A: Resilience is the full integration of our social-emotional skills, from cognitive regulation to emotional processes to interpersonal skills. The more each area is developed, used, and integrated into our daily functioning, the more resilient people become. The strategies in Tip Sheet 17 (p. 144) explain many ways to help our children develop their resilience.

I want to address the second part of the question: coddling fear. Yes, I agree that coddling fear does nothing to increase resilience. In fact, the message it sends to children is just the opposite. By allowing children to avoid the things they fear, parents communicate that they are right to fear those things. Parents say that children can't handle it at all and need parents to run interference for them. This is one of the most destructive things you can do as a parent. That said, there are occasions when your children may not be ready to face everything they fear. You may need to offer support longer than you'd hoped.

Balance the need to support your children and the need to help them face the things they fear. I remember having to find this balance with my own child. She was a young, competitive swimmer. She had been sick for a time and missed a week of practice. When we returned, she had a traumatic experience in the pool that resulted in a temporary, but intense, fear of swimming. More than anything, she wanted me to pull her out of the swim program and allow her to quit. At that time, I didn't believe that was in her best interest—I didn't want her to acquiesce to her fear. I wanted her to overcome it. So we compromised: She wasn't allowed to quit swimming until we could overcome the fear, and I would support her in that process, no matter how long it took.

She went to practice every day, dressed and ready. For the first month or so, she didn't swim at all. We sat by the pool and practiced deep breathing. That was it. Eventually, we were able to do more. She would mentally rehearse swimming, dealing with every terrifying moment in her thoughts. Over time, mental rehearsal lead to swimming a couple of laps and eventually rejoining her team. She overcame her fears.

It wasn't easy. It took patience on everyone's part. But overcoming the fear taught her that she could overcome any fear, no matter how big. It'll always take work, practice, and a little faith. But it will happen.

Q: What can I do as a parent to help my children's schools become more trauma-informed?

A: Schools across the United States have become more and more aware of the impact of trauma and toxic stress on their students. As the awareness has increased, so has the availability of training. To know whether or not your school has had training in becoming trauma-informed, I would start with talking with the teacher and administrator. If there are mental health staff (i.e., counselors, psychologists, or social workers), speak with them as well. They will know the extent to which training has been offered and received by school personnel.

If you find that minimal training has been offered to the staff, or if there is a continued lack of understanding despite training, there are resources you can provide to the school. Tip Sheet 23: Resources for Schools lists several free resources for schools. Provide educators with the list of resources if they need additional help with implementing trauma-informed practices as part of their comprehensive approach to supporting the learning of all students.

> **Tip Sheet 23**
>
> *Resources for Schools*
>
> ---
>
> Need more support? Check these resources for additional information about supporting students experiencing trauma.
>
> o ACEs Too High: https://acestoohigh.com
> o Substance Abuse and Mental Health Services Administration: https://www.samhsa.gov/programs
> o ACEs Connection: https://www.acesconnection.com
> o The National Child Traumatic Stress Network: https://www.nctsn. org/resources

Q: What are some ways I can help my child find a community and feel less alone as a result of their trauma?

A: One of the biggest challenges when people experience trauma is combatting the feelings of isolation and loneliness that often accompany our trauma story. Parents and children often believe that they are the only ones experiencing the event. Or they may feel like they aren't handling things as well as they "should," or as well as others. All of these stories you tell yourself are untrue. Many people experience trauma, and although the experience itself may be unique, the feelings that arise as a result of the event(s) are similar. Finding a community to share your story is the key.

There are a few ways you can find a community—for yourself or for your children. Start with the school counseling staff. If they have support groups, that may be a place to get support for your child. Talk with mental health professionals in your community to see what supports may be available. If the trauma is related to community events, there may be additional resources you can tap into.

Regardless of what resources you are able to access, focus on the feelings you and your children may be experiencing instead of the events themselves. Find commonality with others within those feelings. The more you can recognize—and help your children recognize—that you all share common emotions with others, the more you and your children can find a sense of community with others, no matter what the specific events.

Finally, if you continue to struggle to find a community, start one. Reach out to others. Talk about your story. Help your children to start a community. Volunteer. Give to others who have similar experiences. In all of these ways, you and your children will be able to find connections and community.

Healing the Heart

This chapter of *Healing the Heart* focused on learning to thrive in communities beyond home and school. Attention was given to seeing the strength within the trauma story and using the experience as a force of good in life. The FAQ included questions related to finding a community, moving beyond trauma and helping community organizations—including the medical and emergency response professions—become more trauma-informed.

Heart-Centered Ideas

- The need for community awareness regarding trauma continues, despite decades of research and information.
- Finding the strength pattern within the trauma story is an important step in growth.
- Connections with others is vital to a person's overall well-being.

Healing Actions

- Review Worksheet 4: My Journey Through Trauma (pp. 57–61). What are your key takeaways from the exercise and the book? What questions remain? Jot your answers on the final section of the worksheet.

Chapter 15
Through My Eyes
Conversations With a Trauma-Impacted Adult—*Kendo's Story*

♡

I held many focus groups in preparation for this book, hearing many trauma stories over Zoom, through e-mail, and in person. The story that follows was one that resonated particularly strongly with me. In this story, you will learn about the actual traumatic event, the impact it had to Kendo, and how he moved forward to heal his heart after the event. As with the other stories presented throughout this book, I have changed his name and identifying information. The essence of the story, however, remains true to the original.

♡ ♡ ♡

My name is Kendo and I am 27 years old. When I was 5, my mother killed herself. It was an event that has forever defined my life. Here is my story.

The Event

I was young when my mom died—5, to be exact. But I remember details about that day—all of the details. It started like any other day. I woke, dressed, and went to the kitchen for breakfast. Everything was orderly in my house. No chaos allowed. My mother always had breakfast ready: a bowl of oatmeal or cereal and a piece of fruit. Always the same.

I loved my life. School was fun. I had friends. My parents were strict and expected a lot from me, but I loved them for it. The house was always spotless. Food was made for every meal—no fast food for us. I was the baby of the family. My three older siblings left for school before me on the day of my mother's death, just like always. The weather was cool, winter slowly turning to spring. Mom was quiet as I ate my breakfast. She told me to hurry, that I'd woken late. But I hadn't. It was the same time it always was, not that I could tell her. We didn't question our parents in my house.

The drive to school was uncharacteristically tense. In hindsight, there was so much wrong in the silence that day. But as a 5-year-old child, I didn't understand. The day passed as it always did and at noon, I rushed to find my mom.

But she didn't come.

After all of the other cars were gone, my teacher walked me to the office to call my mom. She had never been late before. I knew something horrible had happened—what else could possibly explain her absence?

Ms. Combs, the lady who sat in the front office, called home. No answer. She tried again. Still no answer. She called my father and said he'd come right away.

The drive home was rushed. Everything about my father was tense: his jaw, the sound of his voice, the lack of eye contact when he picked me up. My world started to fold in on itself. I wanted to cry, even though I didn't know why. Whatever was happening was wrong. I just felt it.

We got home quickly. Mother's car was in the garage. Father's brow furrowed. He told me to stay in the car as he walked into the house.

Time stopped. I heard my father scream. The sound coated my skin. He rushed out, face blanched. Grabbing his phone, he pounded in the numbers 9-1-1. I stepped from the car and Father motioned for me to stay as he explained to the person on the phone that my mother was. . .

Dead.

Suicide—that was the word I remember hearing. Hanging. Definitely dead.

The next moments, days, weeks, are a blur, even now.

The Stories I Told Myself

My father didn't believe in the therapeutic process when I was a child. He still doesn't trust therapists. But he made an exception with me—not that I gave him much of a choice. In the weeks, months, years that followed my mother's suicide, I stopped talking. To everyone. Teachers, counselors, my father—no one heard me speak except for one of my older brothers. He was my interpreter to the world. He told people when I needed something, when I had a question. This arrangement worked everywhere except school; he didn't attend the same school. So I just didn't speak at school.

I had panic attacks almost daily, struggled to form friends, and developed generalized anxiety. I was suffering in silence. I trusted no one, worried about my father and siblings constantly, and waited for my world to implode again. About the only area that wasn't a struggle was my schoolwork. Despite everything, I was highly successful at school. I earned straight As, completed every assignment on time, and excelled in all of my classes.

My academic success comforted my father. It made him proud. In my mind, that would keep him safe. I had told myself that I was to blame for my mother's death, that somehow I wasn't enough. That's why she left me. To keep my father from killing himself, I needed to be the best in everything I tried.

So I studied constantly. I earned full-ride scholarships to four Ivy League schools. I still didn't talk much. My father said I was reserved. He was right, but not for the reasons he thought. I still hadn't received any counseling at this point—not for the first 10 years after my mother's death.

Things changed when I was 17 and starting college.

Healing My Heart

My first step to recovery and healing came during a late night study session at school. College was harder than I'd imagined. With no one to speak for me, and no one who knew what I'd been through, my world finally crashed down. I retreated into my own world. I tried to keep up with my classes, but the work was difficult. I started having nightmares about my mother's death. I shoved my feelings aside and kept trying, harder and harder.

Until I couldn't. And I overdosed on my roommate's medication.

When you're treated for a suicide attempt—that's what they called it—you have no choice but to speak with a therapist. I was hospitalized for 3 weeks. I put school on hold and attended day treatment for another year.

It took time, but I started to talk about my mother's death. I explained that I felt at fault. My therapist helped me to reframe what had happened. I began to see my strength within the pain and sorrow. I recognized the error of my thinking and embraced my inner superhero.

It's taken another 10 years of serious therapy to really move forward. I understand now that my mother's death was about her, not me. I understand that my father's inability to speak about the event was about him, not me. And I now accept that it wasn't my job to take care of anyone other than myself.

I still have occasional nightmares. But I know what to do now, how to move through my emotions.

Mother's suicide will always be a part of my story. But it doesn't define me anymore—it isn't me. It is just one part of a much larger tale of my life.

Kendo's story is a poignant reminder that your trauma story doesn't need to define every aspect of your life. It shapes you and influences you. But it isn't you.

Final Thoughts

$\heartsuit$

Children impacted by adverse childhood experiences and other traumatic events hold a dear place in my heart. Trauma-impacted individuals are kindred spirits, affected by forces beyond their control. Their world often feels scary and unsafe. Their trauma story replays throughout their lives, showing up and influencing their thoughts, feelings, and actions.

Parenting children impacted by trauma is often difficult, especially because parents are affected by trauma as well. Perhaps your child's wounds trigger your own. Maybe you become enmeshed in your child's pain and are forced to relive your own. Or perhaps you just feel overwhelmed and at a loss as to how to help.

I hope that the information, strategies, and stories in this book provide hope and understanding about the impact of trauma and toxic stress, and give you a fresh look into the world of trauma-impacted humans. You may even gain some insight into yourself or the other people in your life.

Throughout the book are tips, strategies, and action items. These may appear overly easy at first glance. Rooted in common sense approaches and familiar language, they are deliberately designed to be easy to use during moments of crisis. This does not mean they are too easy to create long-term impact. Quite the opposite. Every tip, strategy, and recommendation has yielded positive outcomes with numerous children and adults throughout my career and within the research.

To make the most out of the strategies, please adjust them as needed. Not every recommendation will work in every situation. Find the ones that work best for you and start there. But make sure you are well-grounded in the informational part of the book first. This will give you the foundation you need to truly understand the nature of what is happening with your child.

The negative impacts of trauma and toxic stress do not have to be paralyzing. Children and adults can move through the trauma, past the pain, and embrace a life free from all-consuming fear. You and your children can build resiliency and learn to bounce back more quickly from life's ups and downs. You and your children can reverse the negative impact of trauma.

I would love to hear from you and your family about this journey. Contact me with your own stories and suggestions. I can be reached via e-mail at christine@christinefonseca.com or on many social networking sites. Together we can help our children move beyond the negative impact of trauma into a world of hope.

References

American Psychiatric Association. (2013). *Diagnostic and statistical manual of mental disorders* (5th ed.). https://doi.org/10.1176/appi.books.9780890425596

Arneson, T. (2015). *Trauma informed care* [PowerPoint slides]. Temecula, CA.

The Aspen Institute National Commission on Social, Emotional, and Academic Development. (2018). *From a nation at risk to a nation at hope: Recommendations from the national commission on social, emotional, and academic development.* http://nationathope.org/report-from-the-nation-download

Australian Childhood Foundation. (2018). *Making space for learning: Trauma informed practice in schools.* https://professionals.childhood.org.au/app/uploads/2018/08/ACF325-Making-Space-For-Learning-Book-v4.pdf

Biere, J. N., & Lanktree, C. B. (2011). *Treating complex trauma in adolescents and young adults.* SAGE.

Blodgett, C., & Dorado, J. (n.d.). *A selected review of trauma-informed school practice and alignment with educational practice* [White paper].

Brown, D., Anda, R., Edwards, V., Felitti, V., Dubea, S., & Giles, W. (2007). Adverse childhood experiences and childhood autobiographical memory disturbance. *Child Abuse and Neglect, 31*(9), 961–969. https://doi.org/10.1016/j.chiabu.2007.02.011

Brown, L. (2008). *Cultural competence in trauma therapy: Beyond the flashback.* American Psychological Institution.

Burke Harris, N. (2018). *The deepest well: Healing the long-term effects of childhood adversity.* Houghton Mifflin Harcourt.

Calhoun, L. G., & Tedeschi, R. G. (Eds). (2014). *Handbook for post-traumatic growth: Research and practice.* Psychology Press.

Center on the Developing Child. (n.d.). *Resilience.* https://developingchild. harvard.edu/science/key-concepts/resilience

Children's Defense Fund. (2009). *Cradle to prison pipeline fact sheet.* https://www.childrensdefense.org/wp-content/uploads/2018/08/cradle-to-prison-pipeline-overview-fact-sheet-2009.pdf

Cohen, J. A., Mannarino, A. P., & Deblinger, E. (2017). *Treating trauma and traumatic grief in children and adolescents* (2nd ed.). Guilford Press.

Courtois, C. A. (2004). Complex trauma, complex reactions: Assessment and treatment. *Psychotherapy: Theory, Research, Practice, Training, 41*(4), 412–425. https://doi.org/10.1037/0033-3204.41.4.412

Durlak, J. A., Domitrovich, C. E., Weissberg, R. P., & Gullotta, T. P. (Eds.). (2015). *Handbook of social and emotional learning: Research and practice.* Guilford Press.

Felitti, V. J., Anda, R. F., Nordenberg, D., Williamson, D. F., Spitz, A. M., Edwards, V., Koss, M. P., & Marks, J. S. (1998). Relationship of childhood abuse and household dysfunction to many of the leading causes of death in adults: The adverse childhood experiences (ACE) study. *American Journal of Preventative Medicine, 14*(4), 245–258. https://doi.org/10.1016/S0749-3797(98)00017-8

Finkelhor, D., Turner, H. A., Ormrod, R., Hamby, S. L., & Kracke, K. (2009). *Children's exposure to violence: A comprehensive national survey.* U.S. Department of Justice, Office of Justice Programs, Office of Juvenile Justice and Delinquency Prevention.

Fonseca, C. (2015). *Raising the shy child: A parent's guide to social anxiety.* Prufrock Press.

Fonseca, C. (2016). *Emotional intensity in gifted students: Helping kids cope with explosive feelings* (2nd ed.). Prufrock Press.

Fonseca, C. (2017). *Letting go: A girl's guide to breaking free of stress and anxiety.* Prufrock Press.

Fonseca, C. (2018). *Cultivating the resilient classroom: Creating trauma-sensitive environments for students* [PowerPoint slides].

Fonseca, C. (2019). *The caring child: Raising empathetic and emotionally intelligent children*. Prufrock Press.

Friedman, M. J. (n.d.). *Trauma and stress-related disorders in DMS-5* [PowerPoint slides]. https://www.istss.org/ISTSS_Main/media/Documents/ISTSS_DSM-5_Friedman_FINAL_Updated.pdf

Fuld, S. (2018). Autism spectrum disorder: The impact of stressful and traumatic life events and implications for clinical practice. *Clinical Social Work Journal, 46*(3) 210–219. https://doi.org/10.1007/s10615-018-0649-6

Gun Violence Archive. (2019). https://www.gunviolencearchive.org

Gunnar, M., & Quevedo, K. (2007). The neurobiology of stress and development. *Annual Review of Psychology, 58,* 145–173. https://doi.org/10.1146/annurev.psych.58.110405.085605

Herman, J. (2015). *Trauma and recovery: The aftermath of violence – from domestic abuse to political terror*. Basic Books.

Hodas, G. R. (2006). *Responding to childhood trauma: The promise and practice of trauma informed care*. http://www.childrescuebill.org/VictimsOfAbuse/RespondingHodas.pdf

Hughes, M., & Tucker, W. (2018). Poverty as an adverse childhood experience. *North Carolina Medical Journal, 79*(2), 124–126.

Idsoe, T., Dyregrov, A., & Idsoe, E. C. (2012). Bullying and PTSD Symptoms. *Journal of Abnormal Psychology, 40*(6), 901–911. https://doi.org/10.1007/s10802-012-9620-0

Insurance Information Institute. (n.d.). *Facts + statistics: Wildfires.* https://www.iii.org/fact-statistic/facts-statistics-wildfires

Mahoney, J. L., Durlak, J. A., & Weissberg, R. P. (2018). An update on social and emotional learning outcome research. *Phi Delta Kappan, 100,* 18–23.

McGonigal, K. (2015). *The upside of stress: Why stress is good for you, and how to get good at it*. Avery.

The National Child Traumatic Stress Network. (n.d.-a). *Effects.* https://www.nctsn.org/what-is-child-trauma/trauma-types/bullying/effects

The National Child Traumatic Stress Network. (n.d.-b). *Traumatic grief.* https://www.nctsn.org/what-is-child-trauma/trauma-types/traumatic-grief

The National Child Traumatic Stress Network. (2008a). *Child welfare trauma training toolkit: The invisible suitcase.*

The National Child Traumatic Stress Network. (2008b). *Making the connection: Trauma and substance abuse: Fact sheet 1.* https://www.nctsn.org/sites/default/files/assets/pdfs/SAToolkit_1.pdf

The National Child Traumatic Stress Network. (2018). *Child trauma toolkit for educators.* https://www.nctsn.org/resources/child-trauma-toolkit-educators

National Scientific Council on the Developing Child. (2004). *Young children develop in an environment of relationships: Working paper No. 1.* https://developingchild.harvard.edu/resources/wp1

Newell, J. M., & MacNeil, G. A. (2010). Professional burnout, vicarious trauma, secondary traumatic stress, and compassion fatigue: A review of theoretical terms, risk factors, and preventive methods for clinicians and researchers. *Best Practices in Mental Health: An International Journal, 6*(2), 57–68.

Patchin, J. W. (2019). *2019 cyberbullying data.* Cyberbullying Research Center. https://cyberbullying.org/2019-cyberbullying-data

Peña, J., & Chen, M. (2017, November). With great power comes great responsibility: Superhero primes and expansive poses influence prosocial behavior after a motion-controlled game task. *Computers in Human Behavior, 76*, 378–385.

Raja, S. (2012). *Overcoming trauma and PTSD: A workbook integrating skills from ACT, DBT, and CBT.* Harbinger.

Rice, K. F., & Groves B. M. (2005). *Hope and healing: A caregiver's guide to helping young children affected by trauma.* Zero to Three Press.

Scarlet, J. (2019). *Superhero therapy: A hero's journey through acceptance and commitment therapy* [PowerPoint slides].

Sedlak, A. J., & McPherson, K. (2010). *Survey of youth in residential placement: Youth's needs and services.* SYRP Report. Westat.

St. Andrews, A. (2013). *Trauma and resilience: An adolescent provider toolkit.* Adolescent Health Working Group, San Francisco.

Stiglic, N., & Viner, R. M. (2019). Effects of screentime on health and well-being of children and adolescents: a systematic review of reviews. *BMJ Open, 9*(e023191). https://doi.org/10.1136/bmjopen-2018-023191

Substance Abuse and Mental Health Services Administration. (2014). *SAMHSA's concept of trauma and guidance for a trauma-informed approach*. HHS Publication No. (SMA) 14-4884.

Thatcher, R. W., Walker, R. A., & Guidice, S. (1987). Human cerebral hemispheres develop at different rates and ages. *Science, 236*(4805), 1110–1113. https://doi.org/10.1126/science.3576224

The Trevor Project. (2019). *Research brief: Suicide attempts among LGBTQ youth of color*. https://www.thetrevorproject.org/2019/11/26/research-brief-suicide-attempts-among-lgbtq-youth-of-color

Twenge, J. M., & Campbell, W. K. (2018, October). Associations between screen time and lower psychological well-being among children and adolescents: Evidence from a population-based study. *Preventive Medicine Reports, 12*, 271–283. https://doi.org/10.1016/j.pmedr.2018.10.003

Twenge, J. M., Joiner, T. E., Rogers, M. I., & Martin, G. N. (2018). Increases in depressive symptoms, suicide-related outcomes, and suicide rates among U.S. adolescents after 2010 and links to increased new media screen time. *Clinical Psychological Science, 6*(1), 3–17. https://doi.org/10.1177/2167702617723376

U.S. Department of Justice. (2012). *Report of the Attorney General's National Task Force on Children Exposed to Violence*. https://www.justice.gov/sites/default/files/defendingchildhood/cev-rpt-full.pdf

van der Kolk, B. A. (2005). Developmental trauma disorder. *Psychiatric Annals, 35*(5), 401–408.

van der Kolk, B. A. (2014). *The body keeps score: Brain, mind, and body in the healing of trauma*. Penguin Books.

Walkley, M., & Cox, T. L. (2013). Building trauma-informed schools and communities. *Children & Schools, 35*(2), 123–126. https://doi.org/10.1093/cs/cdt007

Washington State Office of Superintendent of Public Instruction. (2011). *Compassionate schools: The heart of learning and teaching*. https://www.k12.wa.us/student-success/health-safety/mental-social-behavioral-health/compassionate-schools-learning-and

Willis, J. (2018). *How emotion impacts the brain's successful learning and what to do about it*. Poster session presented at The Art and Science of Connecting Mind, Body, and Emotions for Student Success Conference, Scotts Valley, CA.

Yates, T. M. (2007). The developmental consequences of child emotional abuse: A neurodevelopmental perspective. *Journal of Emotional Abuse*, 7(2), 9–34. https://doi.org/10.1300/J135v07n02_02

About the Author

$\heartsuit$

Christine Fonseca is a licensed educational psychologist, critically acclaimed author, and nationally recognized speaker on topics related to educational psychology, mental health, giftedness, and using storytelling to heal past wounds. Using her experience consulting and coaching educators and parents, Christine brings her expertise to *Psychology Today*, authoring the parenting blog Parenting for a New Generation. She has written self-help articles for Parents.com, Johnson & Johnson, and *Justine Magazine*. Her appearances on the popular gifted education podcast Mind Matters have been some of its most downloaded episodes.

Christine uses her fictional stories to explore the more complex aspects of humanity through sweeping romances, Gothic thrillers, and psychological horror stories. As a trauma-impacted survivor, Christine believes in the power of storytelling as a key to healing the mind and heart. She delivers soul-centered writing workshops designed to help writers get in touch with their authentic voice and bring that to both their nonfiction and fiction writing.

Christine's critically acclaimed titles include *Emotional Intensity in Gifted Students, Raising the Shy Child, Letting Go: A Girl's Guide to Breaking Free of Stress and Anxiety*, and her highly engaging interactive journals, *The Intense Life Journal* and the *Embrace Intensity Journal*. For more information about Christine or her books, visit her website https://christinefonseca.com or find her on social media.